TURNER

Eric Shanes

STUDIO EDITIONS

LONDON

LDA

For Roger Vignoles and his lady accompanist

Turner published 1990 by Studio Editions Ltd
Princess House, 50 Eastcastle Street
London W1N 7AP, England

ISBN 1–85170–448–5

Printed and bound in Italy

INTRODUCTION

Perhaps no painter in the history of western art evolved over a greater visual span than Turner: if we compare his earliest exhibited masterworks, such as the *Fisherman at Sea* of 1796, with those of the 1840s, such as *The Falls of the Clyde*, it seems hard to credit that they are by the same hand, so vastly do they differ in appearance. This apparent disparity can obscure the profound continuity that underpins Turner's art, just as the dazzling colour and high tonality of the late works can fool us into accepting the notion that the painter shared the ideals of the French Impressionists or that he thought of his painting in its final phase as abstract, which was far from being the case. Instead, that continuity demonstrates how single-mindedly Turner pursued his early goals, and how brilliantly he finally attained them. To trace those aims and their achievement, as well as briefly to recount the artist's life, is the underlying purpose of this book.

Joseph Mallord William Turner was born in Maiden Lane, Covent Garden, London, sometime in late April or early May 1775 (although the artist himself liked to claim that he was born on 23 April, St George's Day and coincidentally Shakespeare's birthday). His father was a wig-maker who had taken to cutting hair after wigs began to go out of fashion in the 1770s. We know little about Turner's mother other than that she was mentally un-balanced, and that her instability was exacerbated by the fatal illness of Turner's younger sister, who died in 1786. Because of the stresses put upon the family by these illnesses, in 1785 Turner was sent to stay with an uncle in Brentford, a small market town to the west of London. It was here that he first went to school. By the following year he was attending school in Margate, a small holiday resort on the Thames estuary to the east of London. Some drawings from those years have survived and they are

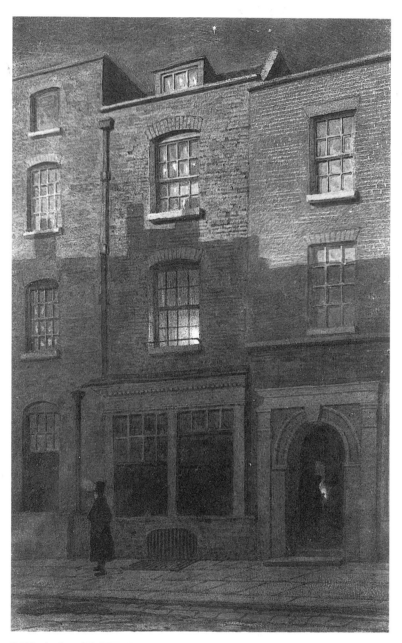

J.W. Archer, J.M.W. Turner's birthplace in Maiden Lane, Covent Garden, *1852*.

remarkably precocious, especially in their grasp of the rudiments of perspective. By the late 1780s Turner was back in London, his formal schooling apparently completed. Around this time he also began working under

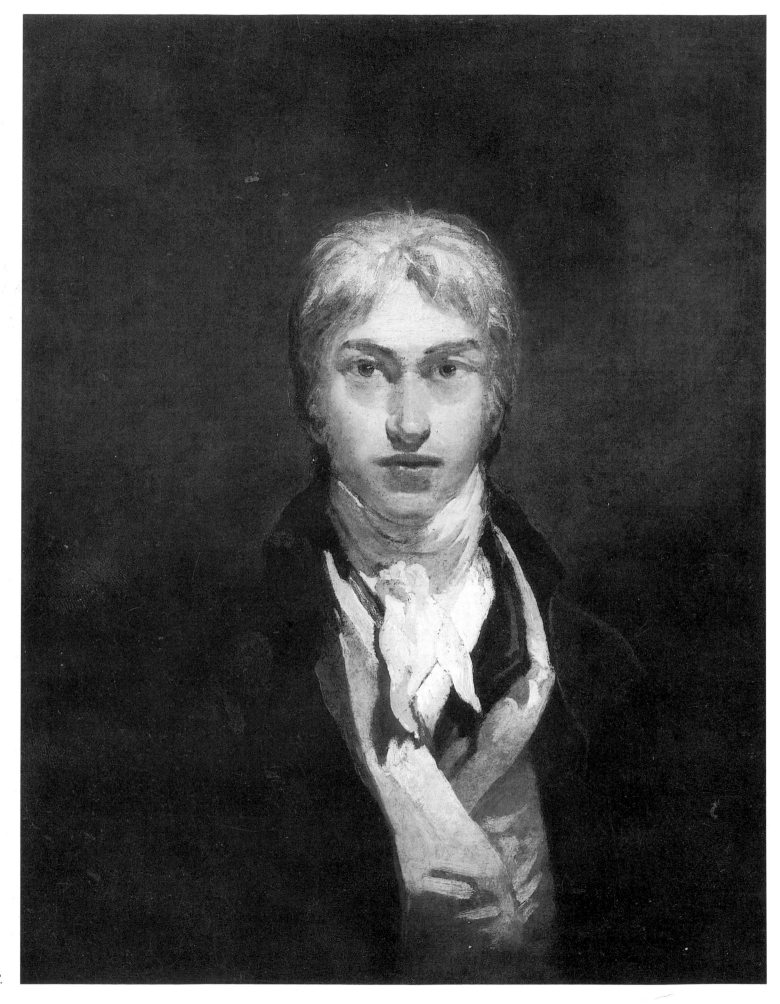

Self-Portrait, *c. 1798.*

various architects or architectural topographers, including Thomas Malton, Jr, whose influence on his work is discernible.

After spending a term as a probationer, on 11 December 1789 Turner was admitted to the Royal Academy Schools, then the only art school in England; the President of the Royal Academy, Sir Joshua Reynolds, chaired the panel that admitted him. At this time painting was not taught in the R.A. Schools (it only appeared on the curriculum in 1816) and students merely learned drawing, at first from plaster casts of antique statuary and then, if deemed good enough — which Turner quickly was — from the nude. Amongst the Visitors or teachers in the life class were History painters such as James Barry and Henry Fuseli whose lofty artistic aspirations would soon rub off on the young Turner.

Naturally, as Turner lived in the days before student grants, he had to earn his keep from the very outset of his career. In 1790 he exhibited at the Royal Academy Exhibition for the first time, and with the exception of a few years he went on annually participating in those shows until 1850. His unusual talents were soon noticed and in 1793 the seventeen-year-old painter was awarded the 'Greater Silver Pallet' for landscape drawing by the Royal Society of Arts. By now Turner was selling works easily, and he supplemented his income throughout the 1790s by giving private lessons. Between 1794 and 1797 he also coloured sketches and prints made by others, on winter evenings meeting with various artists (including another leading young watercolourist, Thomas Girtin) at the home of Dr Thomas Monro, the consultant physician to King George III and the principal doctor at the mental hospital where Turner's mother was later to be treated and where she subsequently died. Monro had established an unofficial artistic 'academy' in his house in Adelphi Terrace overlooking the Thames, and he paid Turner the

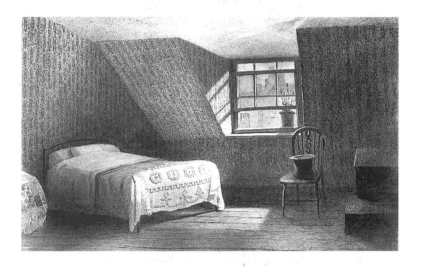

J.W. Archer, Attic in Turner's birthplace in Maiden Lane, Covent Garden, said to have been Turner's first studio, *1852*.

sum of three shillings and sixpence per evening and a supper of oysters to tint copies made in outline by Girtin from works by a number of artists, including Canaletto, Edward Dayes, Thomas Hearne and John Robert Cozens, who at the time was a mental patient under Dr Monro's care. Naturally, Turner absorbed the influence of all these painters, including Girtin, and the breadth of Cozens's landscapes particularly impressed him.

Other important artistic influences upon Turner during the 1790s were Thomas Gainsborough, Michael Angelo Rooker, Philippe Jacques de Loutherbourg, Henry Fuseli and Richard Wilson. Gainsborough's Dutch-inspired landscapes led Turner to a liking for those selfsame types of landscape. Rooker was a fine watercolourist whose control of tone had a long-term influence upon Turner's development as a tonalist and colourist, just as the dramatic role played by his staffage influenced the way that Turner elaborated the human dimensions of the scenes he represented. De Loutherbourg especially influenced the way that Turner painted his figures, varying their style according to the type of image in which they appeared, while Fuseli's heroic style of representing the human form may occasionally be detected in Turner's works. And an appreciation of the pictures of Richard Wilson, who had grafted an Italianate style onto British scenery, soon led Turner to a full appreciation of Claude Gellée (known as Claude Lorrain) who had heavily influenced Wilson and about whom we shall have more to say below. Yet from Turner's mid-teens onwards, one overriding influence came to shape his thinking about his art, and not surprisingly it derived from within the Royal Academy itself, albeit indirectly. This was the influence of Sir Joshua Reynolds.

Turner had attended the last of Reynolds's lectures or discourses in 1790, and through reading the rest of them he seems to have assimilated all of Reynolds's lessons concerning the idealizing aspirations for art that were so eloquently set forth in those fifteen talks. In order to understand Turner's development, it is vital to perceive it in the context of Reynolds's teachings.

In his discourses Reynolds not only set out a comprehensive educational programme for aspiring artists; he also upheld the idealizing tradition of academic art as it had evolved since the Italian Renaissance. This was through the doctrine of 'poetic painting', which held that painting is a humanistic discipline akin to poetry, and that it should concern itself not with the arbitrariness of experience but with universals of behaviour and form. In order to express such fundamentals, painters should attempt to apprehend 'the qualities and causes of things', as well as to synthesize forms so as to make them approximate to 'imagined species' of archetypal form or 'Ideal beauties' (the three foregoing quotations are from Turner himself). To these respective and related ends, after the late 1790s Turner frequently expressed himself through subject-matter drawn from literature and poetry; he filled many of his pictures with all kinds of 'poetic'

devices such as visual metaphors or allegories, allusions, puns and similes, some of which we shall explore in the texts accompanying the individual plates below; gradually he came to express the underlying processes of nature to a matchless degree (leading the critic John Ruskin to devote vast tracts of his book on Turner entitled *Modern Painters* to exploring the painter's grasp of the 'truths' of architecture, geology, the sea, the sky and the other components of a landscape); and from fairly early on in his career Turner came to believe that forms enjoy a metaphysical, eternal and universal existence. From such an apprehension it was easy for the painter to take the short step to believing (as he evidently did shortly before he died) that 'The Sun is God', while because he thought that way we are forced to accept that the near-abstractions of late Turner are no mere painterly abstractions, despite many recent claims to the contrary. Instead, they clearly resulted from attempts to represent the metaphysical power embodied in light, if not even the divinity itself.

Reynolds thought landscape painting to be a fairly simple-minded genre because it had never said much about the human condition, which for him was the principal subject of high art. Equally, he accorded landscape painting a rather low place in his artistic scheme of things quite simply because landscapists were mainly beholden to chance: if they visited a place when, say, it happened to be raining, then that was how they would be forced to represent it. Instead, Reynolds recommended the practice of landscapists like Claude Lorrain, who had synthesized into fictive and ideal scenes the most attractive features of several places as viewed in the best of weather and lighting conditions, thus transcending the arbitrary. Although Turner gave more weight to representing individual places than Reynolds had allowed for, nonetheless in all other respects he adopted the

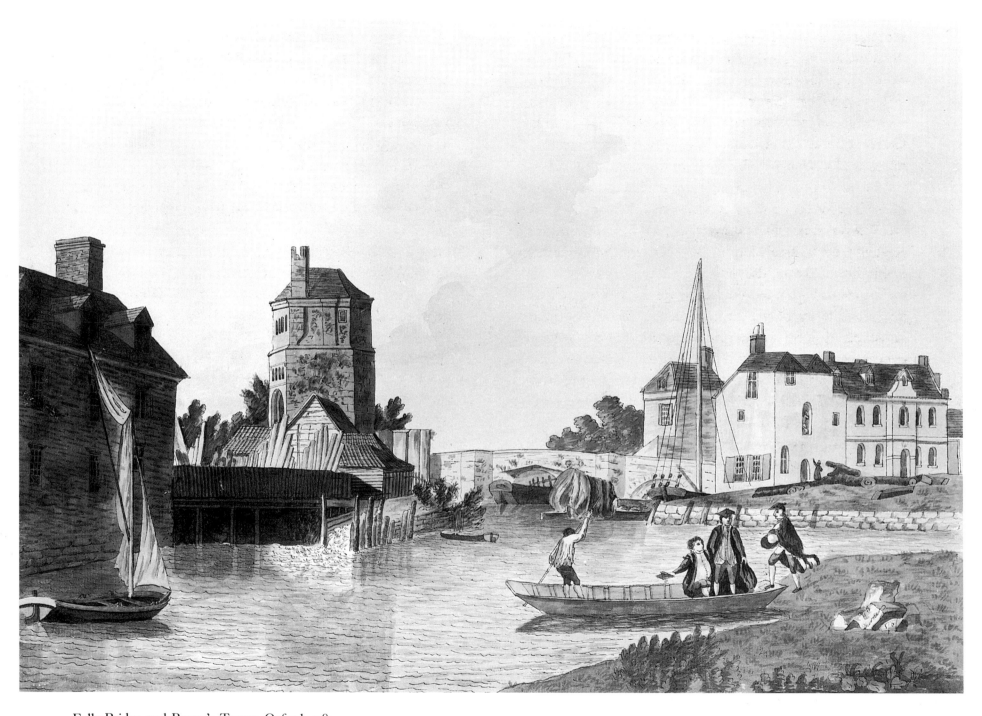

Folly Bridge and Bacon's Tower, Oxford, *1787*.

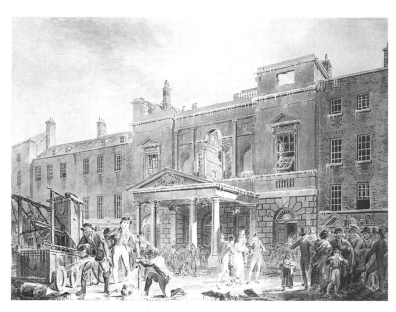

The Pantheon, the morning after the fire, *R.A. 1792.*

synthesizing practice recommended by Reynolds, for as he was to state around 1810:

> To select, combine and concentrate that which is beautiful in nature and admirable in art is as much the business of the landscape painter in his line as in the other departments of art.

To such an end Turner would often freely alter or omit anything in a particular scene that did not accord with his imaginative demands — so that sometimes his landscapes bore little resemblance to the actuality of a place — while unusual or particularly lovely weather effects that had been witnessed in one place could be transposed into representations of others. And always Turner employed to the full his unusual powers of mental association to link things. He made clear his belief in the supremacy of the imagination in a paraphrase of Reynolds that stands at the very core of his artistic thinking:

> . . . it is necessary to mark the greater from the lesser truth: namely the larger and more liberal idea of nature from the comparatively narrow and confined; namely that which addresses itself to the imagination from that which is solely addressed to the Eye.

Yet this does not mean that Turner neglected the eye. He was an inveterate sketcher, and there are over 300 sketchbooks in the Turner Bequest, incorporating over 10,000 individual sketches. Often he would sketch a place even if he had sketched it several times before, and by doing so he not only mastered the appearances of things but also honed his unusually retentive memory, which was an important tool for the idealizing artist, inasmuch as memory sifts the essential from the unimportant. Turner's principal method of studying appearances and still allowing himself room for imaginative manoeuvre was to sketch a view in outline, omitting any effects of weather, light or even human figures and other animal inhabitants (if needed, these ancillaries would be studied separately) and then to return to the sketch at a later date, supplying the ancillaries mainly from memory and/or the imagination. Turner kept all his sketchbooks as a reference library, and sometimes he would return to them as much as forty years later in order to obtain factual information for an image. This practice began in the early 1790s, and it is easy to perceive how it grew directly from the idealizing admonitions of Reynolds.

Moreover, as well as ideal 'imitation' — the creation of perfected notions of form, which by definition included the expression of the 'qualities and causes' of things — Reynolds had also advocated artistic imitation, the absorption of the qualities of the finest masters of past art through imitating them stylistically. Here too Turner followed Reynolds assiduously. Throughout his life he emulated the pictorial formulations of a vast range of past (and present) masters, from Titian, Raphael and Salvator Rosa in the Italian school, to Claude, Nicolas Poussin and Watteau in the French school, to Rembrandt, Cuyp, van de Velde and Backhuizen in the Dutch school, to any

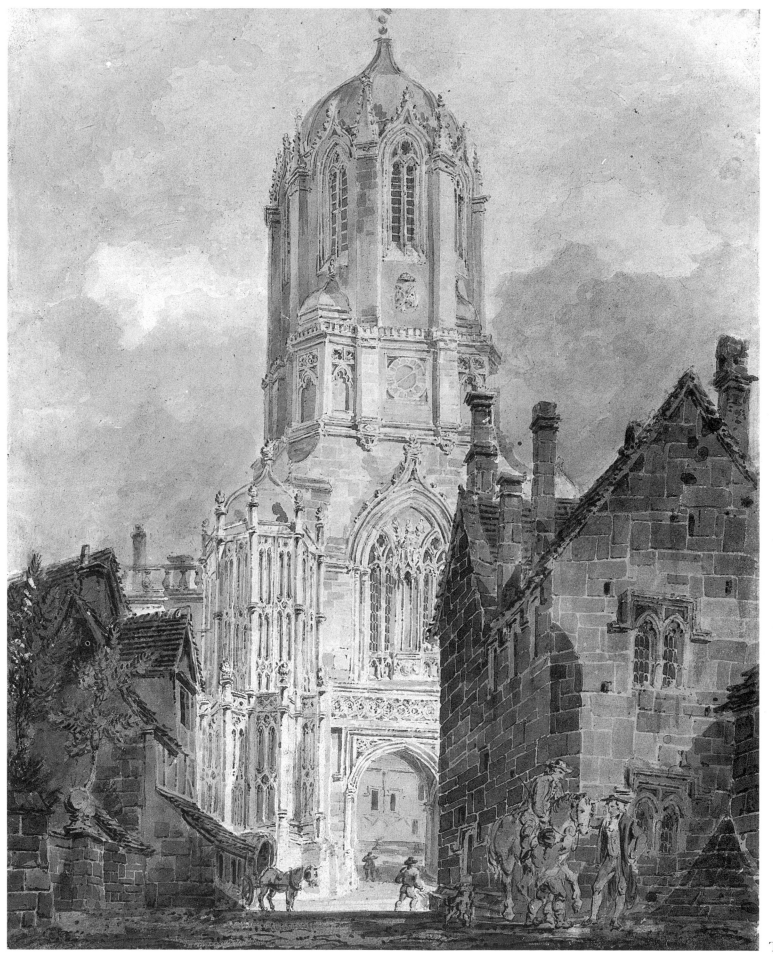

Tom Tower, Oxford, *c. 179*

number of his contemporaries in the English school. Such emulation was not the sign of any imaginative deficiency in Turner, nor was it a matter of somebody who supposedly had an inferiority complex pitting himself *against* his betters, as has often been suggested. Turner was merely following Reynolds's teachings and example, and it is a mark of his creative vision that whomsoever he emulated, the results always ended up looking thoroughly Turnerian (even if they did fall short of their models in terms of quality).

In 1791 Turner made the first of his great many sketching tours; during the 1790s alone he ranged over the south of England, the Midlands, the north of England and the Lake District, as well as making five tours of Wales in search of the kind of scenery that had been pictorialized by Richard Wilson. On each tour he would fill a number of sketchbooks with dry topographical studies and the occasional watercolour, from which he would work up elaborate paintings and watercolours when back in London.

A surviving memoir of Turner on his sketching tour of Wales and the West Country in 1798 makes his priorities very clear:

> I recollect Turner as a plain uninteresting youth both in manners and appearance, he was very careless and slovenly in his dress, not particular what was the colour of his coat or clothes, and was anything but a nice looking young man . . . He would talk of nothing but his drawings, and of the places to which he should go for sketching. He seemed an uneducated youth, desirous of nothing but improvement in his art . . .

This view of the young painter seems to have been a general one, for it was echoed by the topographical artist Edward Dayes whose perception of Turner was published in 1805: 'The man must be loved for his works; for his person is not striking nor his conversation brilliant.'

Although Turner's intellect was enormous, his patchy education and wholehearted commitment to his art meant that he cut a poor figure socially, and although in time he would gain in social confidence, his remarkable emotional sensitivity was the cause of a corresponding vulnerability (which may have derived from unhappy childhood experiences brought about by the instability of his mother), and these meant that he always maintained his emotional defences until he felt that he could fully trust people not to hurt him. When he did trust them, however — and he always trusted the company of children — then a completely different side of his personality could emerge. This can be seen in another memoir of Turner as a young man, by his lifelong friend Clara Wells:

> Of all the light-hearted, merry creatures I ever knew, Turner was the most so; and the laughter and fun that abounded when he was an inmate in our cottage was inconceivable, particularly with the juvenile members of the family. I remember coming in one day after a walk, and when the servant opened the door the uproar was so great that I asked the servant what was the matter. 'Oh, only the young ladies (my young sisters) playing with the young gentleman (Turner), Ma'am.' When I went into the sitting room, he was seated on the ground, and the children were winding his ridiculously long cravat round his neck; he said, 'See here, Clara, what these children are about!'

Turner's 'home from home' in the cottage of Clara Wells's father, William Wells, at Knockholt in Kent, was the first of several that he enjoyed throughout his life, and by the end of the 1790s, as the insanity of his mother intensified, it must have seemed a vital means of escape to him. And as soon as he could afford it the painter moved from the parental abode in Maiden Lane, in late 1799 obtaining rooms at 64 Harley Street in a house that eventually he would take over completely.

From the mid-1790s onwards Turner's idealism was already finding expression in his representation of architecture, as is demonstrated by the 1794 watercolour of *St Anselm's Chapel, Canterbury* reproduced on p. 47. In works like this we can detect a total comprehension of the underlying dynamics of man-made structures, over and above a grasp of their surface appearances. Within a short time such apprehensions would extend to the depiction of geological structures, and Turner saw a profound linkage between man-made architecture and natural architecture, not only believing that the principles of the one are based upon the laws of the other, but even that a universal, metaphysical geometry underlies both. This belief was fuelled from the mid-1790s onwards by a close reading of poetry, most particularly the verse of Mark Akenside, whose long poem 'The Pleasures of the Imagination' states a Platonic idealism with which Turner completely identified, with momentous results for his art.

From the mid-1790s onwards we can equally detect Turner's total apprehension of the fundamentals of hydrodynamics. The *Fishermen at Sea* of 1796 demonstrates how intently the painter had already been looking at wave formation, reflectivity and the underlying motion of the sea. From this time onwards his depiction of the sea would become ever more masterly, soon achieving a mimetic and expressive power that is unrivalled in the history of marine painting. There have been and are many marine painters who have gone beyond Turner in the degree of photographic realism they have brought to the depiction of the sea, but none of them has come within miles — nautical miles, naturally — of his expression of the behaviour of water. By 1801, when Turner exhibited 'The Bridgewater Seapiece', his grasp of such dynamics was complete, and by that time also the painter had simultaneously begun to master the ideality of clouds, making apparent the fundamental dynamics of meteoro-

logical form, a comprehension that he fully attained by the mid-1800s. Only his trees remained somewhat mannered during the 1800s, but between 1809 and 1813 Turner gradually discovered how to impart his understanding of the 'qualities and causes' of trees, something he achieved by replacing a rather old-fashioned mannerism in his depictions of boughs and foliage with a greater sinuousness of line and an increased structural complexity. By 1815 that transformation was completed, and during the next two decades, in works like the *Mortlake Terrace* of 1826 (reproduced on p. 93), Turner's trees became perhaps the loveliest and most expressive arboreal forms anywhere in art.

The 1796 *Fishermen at Sea* was also Turner's first exhibited oil painting, and it demonstrates his natural proficiency in the medium. By 1796, of course, he had already mastered watercolour, and indeed, there was henceforth nothing that he could not attain in such a drawing technique, being capable of investing it with the same powers of expression and representation that are usually to be found only in oil paint. Similarly, in his oil paintings the artist increasingly attained the kind of brilliance and luminosity that are more usually to be seen only in watercolour.

Primarily Turner chose to employ watercolour rather than oil paint because of the cultural roles of the two media rather than because there was much he could achieve in one of them and not the other. Watercolour was fast to work with but intimate in response and public appeal; oil paint was slower-drying but more highly regarded culturally and more publicly assertive through its capacity for deployment over much larger surfaces. Ultimately, however, Turner enjoyed an equal sureness in both media, and initially that certainty was acquired from the practice of watercolour in the 1790s when he spent so many hours tinting and colouring architectural

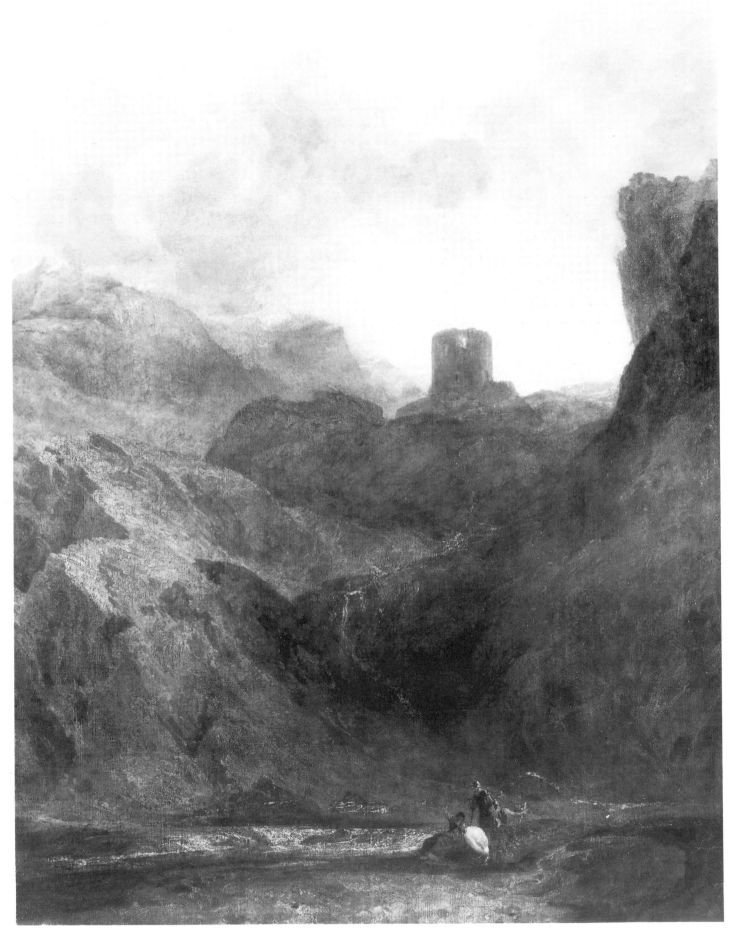

Dolbadern Castle, North Wales, *R.A. 1800.*

elevations and views. These provided Turner not only with a sense of the precise tonal values of things but also with an immensely firm control over both subtle and broad tonal washes. In time, the painter's control of tone would have the most profound effect upon his abilities as a colourist, allowing him to achieve a brilliance of colour without necessarily having to use bright colours at all. Moreover, Turner never rested on his laurels as far as his painting technique was concerned. In order to extend himself, often he would set himself technical challenges, such as choosing for a set of watercolours an unfamiliar kind of support like blue or grey paper. In some of his late works Turner's trust in new materials was misplaced, with disastrous results, but in the main his works are technically sound, and when he was especially inspired, as with *The Fighting 'Temeraire'* of 1839, he would go to great lengths to paint the work as carefully as possible.

In 1798 a change in the rules governing the Royal Academy Exhibitions allowed artists to include quotations from poetry alongside the titles of their works in the exhibition catalogues. Turner immediately embarked upon a public examination of the interdependent roles of painting and poetry, how each discipline could support the other and where their individual powers resided. In 1798 he appended poetic quotations (including verses by John Milton and James Thomson that identify the sun with God) to the titles of five works, in some to test the ways that painting can realize and/or heighten the imagery of poetry, in others to explore the way that poetic imagery can extend the associations of what we see, and thus move us into realms of imaginative response that we cannot reach unaided. In 1799 Turner took this latter process a stage further, employing alongside the titles of five works a poetry that is particularly rich in metaphors in order similarly to extend the images imaginatively into areas that pictorialism cannot explore without verbal help.

And in 1800, with two views of Welsh castles (one of which, *Dolbadern Castle*, is reproduced here), Turner reversed the foregoing procedure by quoting only descriptive poetry that is devoid of metaphors, and instead incorporated the metaphors *into* the images themselves, thus completing the process of integrating painting and poetry whilst greatly extending the ability of visual images to convey meanings. Thereafter, Turner did not again quote poetry in connection with the titles of his works in the exhibition catalogues for another four years, although when he did so it was to state the internal responses of the people he portrayed, something that again painting cannot fully express unaided by words. This exploration of the respective powers of painting and poetry was to be of inestimable value to Turner, for he continued to benefit from his discoveries throughout the rest of his career.

Turner's investigation of the mechanisms by which pictorial meanings are communicated was equally helped by the close study he made around 1799 of the imagery of Claude Lorrain. He may have been led to undertake such a detailed analysis through being particularly struck by two paintings by Claude. One was the *Landscape with the Father of Psyche sacrificing at the Milesian Temple of Apollo* which had just been brought to Britain from Italy, and in front of which Turner was recorded as being 'both pleased and unhappy while He viewed it, — it seemed to be beyond the power of imitation'. The other picture was a seaport scene that belonged to the wealthy London collector John Julius Angerstein. Turner responded to this painting in a rather dramatic (and wholly characteristic) fashion:

When Turner was very young he went to see Angerstein's pictures. Angerstein came into the room while the young painter was looking at the Sea Port by Claude, and spoke to him. Turner was awkward, agitated, and burst into tears. Mr Angerstein enquired the cause and pressed for an answer, when Turner said passionately, 'Because I shall never be able to paint anything like that picture.'

Turner's close study of Claude around 1799 was undertaken not only by looking carefully at paintings like these, but also by scrutinizing two books of prints entitled 'Liber Veritatis' ('Book of Truth'), a set of 200 mezzotints engraved by Richard Earlom after drawings made by Claude upon the completion of each of his paintings. Claude greatly utilized visual metaphor, whereby something we see stands for something unseen, and there can be no doubt that Turner recognized some of his metaphors, for in time he emulated them very closely indeed. Turner's responsiveness to Claude — whose influence was perhaps the greatest of all the many painterly influences he assimilated — had a very profound effect upon his expressions of meaning, just as it determined the development of his mature style and imagery.

Throughout the 1790s Turner had been obtaining better and better prices for his works as demand increased; an indication of that popularity may be gauged from the fact that by July 1799 he had orders for no less than sixty watercolours awaiting fulfilment. And his growing status in the market place was matched by his growing esteem within the Royal Academy, a recognition that was made official on 4 November 1799 when he was elected an Associate Royal Academician. This was a necessary preliminary to becoming a full Academician, and Turner would not have long to wait before receiving the higher honour.

At the Royal Academy in 1801 he made a major contribution towards such an elevation when he exhibited his greatest seascape to date, the *Dutch Boats in a gale: fishermen endeavouring to put their fish on board*, also known as 'The Bridgewater Seapiece' after the Duke of Bridgewater who had commissioned it. The picture caused a sensation, and this boost to Turner's reputation importantly contributed to his being elected a full Royal Academician on 12 February 1802 at the age of just twenty-six. Becoming an Academician granted Turner election to a very exclusive club indeed, and one with the best of cultural and economic advantages, that of having a place in which automatically to display his works publicly every year without having to submit them to a selection committee.

In the summer of 1801 Turner made an extensive tour of Scotland, and this was the most ambitious trip he had undertaken so far. After his return he showed his Scottish drawings to his fellow landscapist, the painter and diarist Joseph Farington, R.A., who noted early in 1802 that:

> Turner thinks Scotland a more picturesque country to study in than Wales, the lines of the mountains are finer, and the rocks of larger masses.

But later in the same year Turner had the opportunity to study mountains that greatly dwarfed those of Scotland. In March 1802 a peace was signed between Britain and France, and this interruption of the war between the two nations that had already lasted for almost nine years allowed Turner to go abroad for the first time. He knew that to see truly majestic scenery in Europe you must go to the Swiss alps, and that was where he made for in the summer of 1802, exploring some of the western cantons and the northern reaches of the Val d'Aosta before making his way up to Schaffhausen on the Rhine and thence to Basel and Paris where he stopped off to see the Louvre. In Paris Turner met Farington, and told him that in Switzerland he had suffered 'much fatigue from walking, and often experienced bad food & lodgings. The weather was very fine. He saw very fine Thunder Storms among the Mountains.' In the Louvre Turner closely scrutinized works by Poussin, Titian and others, although

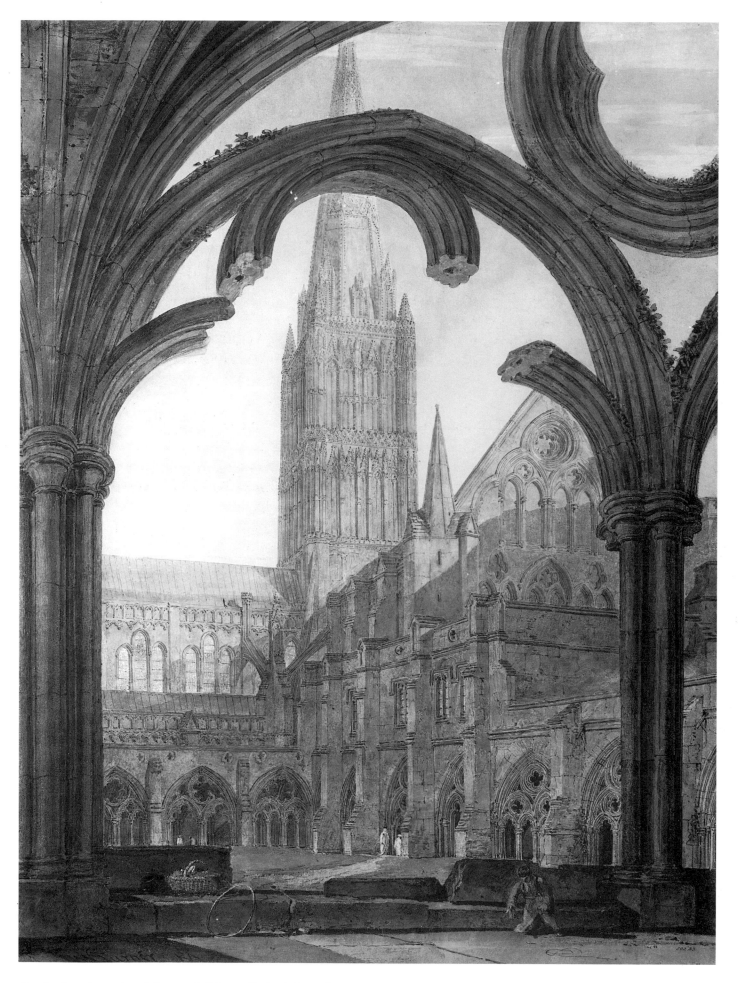

South view from the cloisters, Salisbury Cathedral, *c. 1802.*

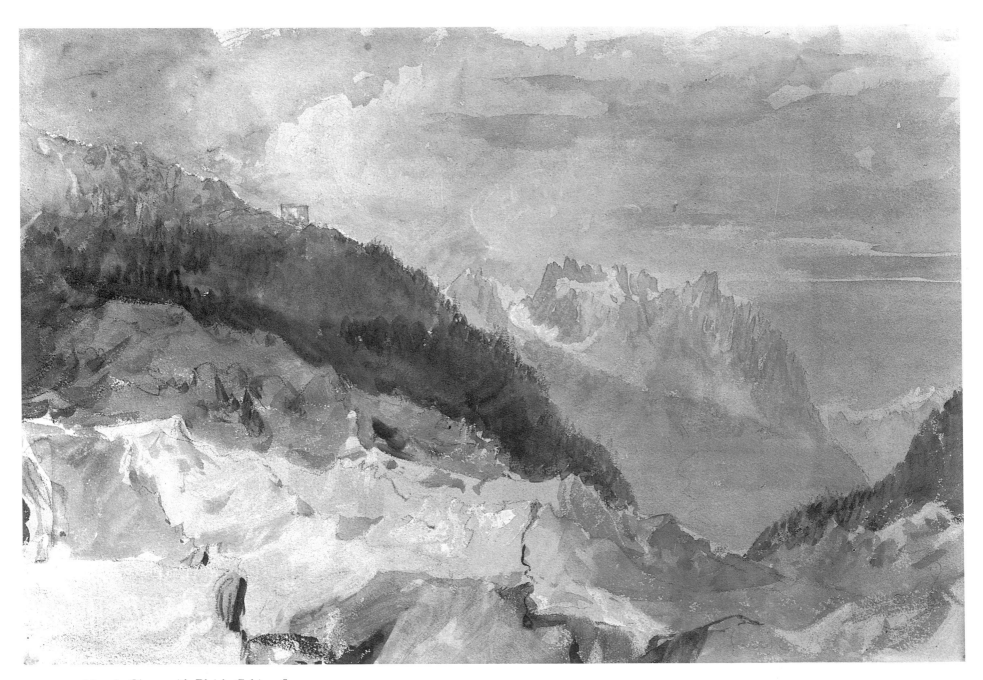

Mer de Glace, with Blair's Cabin, *1802*.

unfortunately the numerous Claudes in the collection do not seem to have been on view.

On his return Turner elaborated his responses to Swiss scenery, and during the following winter he also produced an impressive painting of the view from Calais Pier looking across the English Channel, a work in which he may have been making a subtle anti-French statement. Such a secondary purpose was perhaps natural, given that while Turner was busy on the picture all the talk in Britain was of the resumption of hostilities with France.

By this time Turner had become a father. Although he always refused to marry, he is known to have sired two daughters, Evelina and Georgiana, and it has been generally assumed that their mother was a Mrs Sarah Danby, the widow of a London composer of glees and catches, John Danby, who had died in 1798. However, recent research has thrown severe doubt on this assumption, and it seems much more likely that the mother of Turner's daughters was Sarah's niece, Hannah Danby, who is known to have served Turner as the housekeeper of one of his London residences from the 1820s onwards and to whom the painter left a substantial legacy in his will. Nothing is known of Hannah Danby's personality or her looks as a young woman, but later in life she seems to have been afflicted with a skin disease, so that she appeared rather repulsive.

Turner was increasingly busy during the 1800s. In 1803 he began to construct a gallery for displaying his works in his house in Harley Street, apparently because the contentious atmosphere in the Royal Academy wearied him, although he went on steadily exhibiting there. The first show in Turner's Gallery opened in April 1804, with as many as thirty works on display. Further annual exhibitions were held there regularly until 1810, and then more spasmodically over the following decade.

By the late 1800s Turner was also residing for parts of

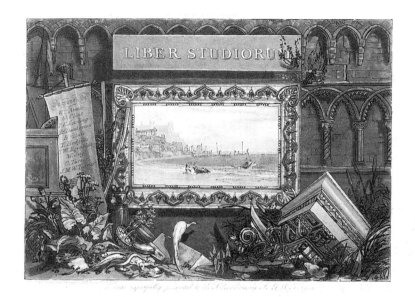

Frontispiece of 'Liber Studiorum', *1812*.

the year outside London proper, first at Sion Ferry House in Isleworth, west of London, and then, after 1806, nearby at Hammersmith, where he went on staying until 1811 when he began building a small villa called Solus Lodge (which he later renamed Sandycombe Lodge) in Twickenham, also to the west of London. He designed this latter house himself and it is still standing, although it has been somewhat altered down the years. During this decade Turner did little touring, being extremely busy producing works for his own gallery and for the Academy, as well as innumerable watercolours on commission. His clientele continued to swell, and included some of the leading collectors of the day such as Sir John Leicester (later Lord de Tabley) and Walter Fawkes. The latter was a bluff, no-nonsense and very liberal-minded Yorkshireman whose home, Farnley Hall, near Leeds, Turner began visiting around 1808. Fawkes was perhaps the closest to Turner of all his patrons, and the painter went on regularly visiting Farnley until the mid-1820s, becoming very much a part of the Fawkes family.

In 1806 Turner also embarked upon a major set of engravings, the preliminary etchings for which he drew himself. This was the 'Liber Studiorum' ('Book of Studies') which was not only intentionally similar in title to the Claude-Earlom 'Liber Veritatis', but which was made in the identical medium of mezzotint. Originally there were to have been 100 prints in the 'Liber Studiorum' but by 1819 only 71 of them had been published and the project petered out, although drawings or proofs of the remaining designs have survived. Turner was clearly inspired by his own close study of the Claude-Earlom model to offer his 'Liber Studiorum' as a similar inspiration to others. To further that didactic aim he broke its subjects down into categories, namely Architectural, Marine, Mountainous, Historical, Pastoral and Elevated Pastoral, the last category being employed to differentiate the noble and somewhat mythical type of pastoralism found in the works of Claude and Poussin from the ruddy and farmyard type found in Lowlands painting and/or reality.

As well as being drawn to Ideal art during these years Turner also made clear his identification with other aesthetic concepts, as well as with less exalted types of imagery. To take the first, around 1800 the painter was clearly attracted to the notion of the Sublime, that power of spatial enormity in reality or amplification through art which produced sensations of grandeur, mystery and even horror through the reduction of the spectator to physical insignificance. At the turn of the new century Turner's identification with sublimity led him to paint a number of works in an upright format, scenes in which the spectator is located at a low viewpoint so that we are overwhelmed by the scale and grandeur of the settings they project, as well as by the mysterious darkness that fills many of them.

Perhaps the greatest picture Turner painted in the Sublime mode during these years was the *Dolbadern Castle* of 1800, although here the painter put the Sublime at the disposal of the poetic by altering the topography of the scene so as to increase our sense of physical enclosure and thus force us to share the experience of the prisoner who is the protagonist of the work. Such a direction of the physical qualities of a landscape to extending human experience clearly indicates Turner's humanistic priorities as a result of his wholehearted identification with the theory of poetic painting. He never lost his feeling for the grandeur, mystery and fear-inducing powers of external nature but increasingly, as his palette lightened in the decade after 1800 and his desire to elaborate his academic idealism increased, Turner eschewed upright formats and pictorial darkness as economical ways to create mystery. Instead he imparted grandeur and mysteriousness by means of adjustments of internal scale, light tones, bright colours and vivacious forms, something far more difficult to bring off.

And Turner also consciously evolved an anti-ideal figuration. For Reynolds, as well as for a host of other academic theorists, the supreme purpose of poetic painting was to exalt the human form, to project an ideal beauty of humanity. But Turner rejected that central tenet of the theory of poetic painting. Even by 1801, when he completed the 'Bridgewater Seapiece', he had drawn upon the example of Lowlands painting for the formation of his figures, especially modelling them upon those by David Teniers the younger who had a large following in Britain for the wittiness of his intentionally boorish people. In impressive marine paintings such as the 'Bridgewater Seapiece', *Calais Pier* of 1803 and *The Shipwreck* of 1805, Turner intentionally aped the look of Teniers's figures in order to state the central moral contrast of his art as far as humanity is concerned: the

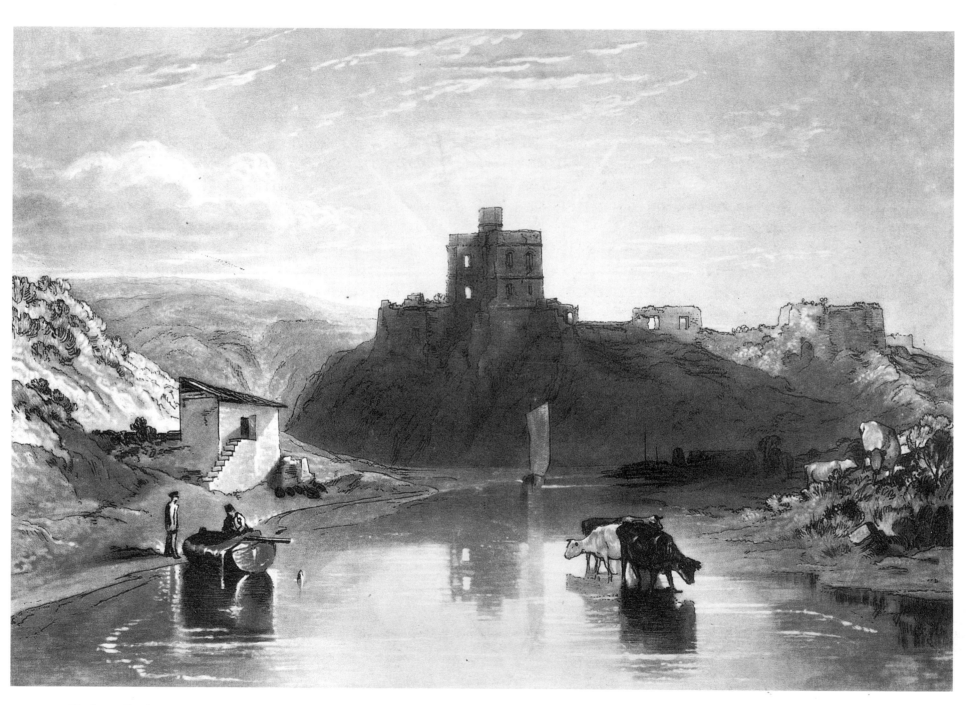

Norham Castle on the Tweed, *engraving for the 'Liber Studiorum',*
1816.

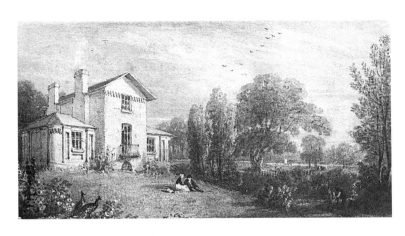

William Havell, Sandycombe Lodge, Twickenham, the Seat of J.M.W. Turner, *R.A., c. 1814.*

world around us is immense, beautiful or ferocious, and eternally renewing itself, whereas man is tiny and of very limited lifespan and powers. For Turner our hubris in pitting ourselves against external nature was clearly a comic as well as a cosmic matter, and to point up that comicality he made his figures look as gauche, crude, child-like, or even doll-like as possible, as Teniers and other painters influenced by the Flemish artist (such as de Loutherbourg) had done, thus enforcing the maximum contrast between humanity and nature beyond us. In this respect Turner consciously turned his back on the major aspect of the academic idealism propounded by Reynolds, the formation of beautified human archetypes. Instead Turner created an inverted, anti-heroic and 'low' archetype to stand for humanity, but one that nonetheless represented something archetypical in mankind in an age in which the majority of people lived tragically short and brutalized lives.

At the very end of 1807 Turner took yet another step that was to have enormously beneficial results for his art: he accepted the position of Royal Academy Professor of Perspective. The post had been vacant for some years, and between 1807 and 1811 (when he delivered his first lecture) the painter embarked upon a rigorous study programme, reading or re-reading over 70 books on art and aesthetics. Turner went on delivering the lectures spasmodically until 1828 (although he did not resign the position until 1838), and their texts are now in the British Library. They make it clear that Turner did not limit himself to an analysis of perspective. Instead he surveyed his art in its entirety, making his identification with the academic theory of poetic painting and its intrinsic idealism apparent in the process but equally mystifying his audiences, who wanted to learn something less exalted, namely the basics of perspective itself.

It is easy to detect a visual sharpening of Turner's idealism in the years after 1811, and clearly the lectures contributed greatly to that heightened sensibility. One such augmentation took place in Turner's watercolours and stemmed jointly from yet another discovery that the artist had made in 1811, namely the expressive power of line engraving (whereby an image is etched and cut into a metal plate, and reproduces the design solely through varying intensities of line). Turner had made watercolours to be copied as line engravings since the early 1790s but in 1811 he was astounded by the degree of tonal beauty and expressiveness attained by one of his engravers, John Pye, in the engraving of *Pope's Villa at Twickenham* (the painting of which is discussed below) and this made him receptive to having more of his works reproduced in this way. As a result, shortly afterwards he welcomed the proposal that he should make a large set of watercolours of the scenery of the southern coast of England for subsequent line-engraving. The 'Southern Coast' project was only completed in the mid-1820s but it was instrumental in leading Turner to express more consistently the essentials of place, those underlying social, cultural, historical and economic factors that had determined their existence or which still governed life there. In time Turner would create several hundreds of watercolours for similar schemes, and in a great many of them he would display the utmost ingenuity in subtly elaborating the truths of place.

In 1812 Turner exhibited an unusually important picture at the Royal Academy, *Snow Storm: Hannibal and his Army crossing the Alps*. Such a subject had intrigued the painter since the late 1790s when he had copied a portrayal by J.R. Cozens of Hannibal looking down into Italy, a work that is unfortunately now lost. Yet the actual inspiration for a painting on that subject only came to Turner late in the summer of 1810 when he stayed at Farnley Hall. One day he called Fawkes's son, Hawksworth Fawkes, over to the doorway of the house and said:

'Hawkey! Hawkey! Come here! Come here! Look at this thunder-storm. Isn't it grand? — isn't it wonderful? — isn't it sublime?' All this time he was making notes of its form and colour on the back of a letter. I proposed some better drawing-block, but he said it did very well. He was absorbed — he was entranced. There was the storm rolling and sweeping and shafting out its lightning over the Yorkshire hills. Presently the storm passed, and he finished.

'There! Hawkey,' said he. 'In two years you will see this again, and call it "Hannibal Crossing the Alps".' This story indicates how far Turner characteristically subordinated the sublime to the poetic, for he synthesized his landscape as Reynolds had recommended by marrying a Yorkshire storm to a Swiss alpine scene and immediately put both at the service of a 'poetic' theme. Sublimity was not an end for Turner but merely a beginning.

With *Hannibal and his Army crossing the Alps* Turner also made an important debut in 1812. Although the painter had been appending lines of verse to the titles of his pictures in the exhibition catalogues since 1798, and some of it may have been of his own devising, in 1812 and

for the first time, he added lines that were openly by himself. These verses were drawn from a 'poem' entitled 'Fallacies of Hope' that only ever seems to have existed in the exhibition catalogues. Yet its title, and often the verses themselves, indicate Turner's view that all hopes of successfully defying the forces of external nature, of overcoming the contradictions of human nature, and of religious redemption, are fallacious. Turner continued to state such morals right up until 1850, the last year in which he exhibited at the Academy. In the case of *Hannibal* the verse reminds us of the central irony of Hannibal's life, that for all his immense and successful efforts to cross the alps into Italy, eventually the Carthaginian general would entirely nullify his triumphant achievement by becoming ensconced in idleness and luxury at Capua, thus frittering away his chances of defeating the Romans. Clearly it was an irony that was directed at Turner's fellow empire-building countrymen, warning of the perils that awaited them if they similarly neglected their duty to serve the needs of the state and of each other. The notion that each citizen should eschew self-interest, vanity and luxury in pursuit of the common welfare, was frequently encountered in eighteenth-century Augustan poetry, whence Turner undoubtedly derived it, and he was to state that moral repeatedly after 1812 in pictures not only of Carthage but also of other great empires such as Greece, Rome and Venice whose downfall because of individual self-interest might similarly serve to warn England. Indeed, moralism became increasingly important in Turner's work after 1812, as the painter put into practice his belief, stated in a letter of the previous year, that it is the duty of an artist to act equally as a moral seer.

The *Snow Storm: Hannibal and his Army crossing the Alps* received some very favourable comments. For example, the American painter Washington Allston called it a 'wonderfully fine thing', declaring that Turner was 'the greatest painter since the days of Claude'. Yet Turner's art was not always received so rapturously. Throughout the 1800s it had been severely criticized by the influential connoisseur, painter and collector Sir George Beaumont, who professed to be alarmed by the liberties that Turner took with appearances, and by the increasingly high tonalities visible in his works. Beaumont was probably secretly jealous of Turner's great artistic success, having himself once been called the 'head of the landscape' [school], an honour that Turner had easily assumed during the 1790s and 1800s, and he did his utmost to discourage other collectors from buying works by the younger painter. Turner was understandably annoyed by this, although by the early 1810s he already had a loyal following who were prepared to pay high prices for his pictures.

In 1813 Turner exhibited at the Royal Academy an unusually fine rural scene, *Frosty Morning*, as well as his dramatic riposte to Poussin's *Deluge*, a picture he had painted some years earlier. In 1814 he exhibited two works, one of which, *Apullia in search of Appullus*, contained a veiled attack on Sir George Beaumont. And in 1815 Turner exhibited two of his greatest paintings to date, *Crossing the Brook* and *Dido building Carthage; or, the Rise of the Carthaginian Empire*, which is discussed in more detail below. Turner particularly esteemed *Dido*, and when he came to draw up the first version of his will in 1829 he requested that the canvas should be used as his winding-sheet upon his death and even asked one of his executors, Francis Chantrey, whether that condition of the will would be followed. To his eternal credit Chantrey replied that it would but that 'as soon as you are buried I will see you taken up and unrolled', whereupon Turner amended his will and instead left the painting to the National Gallery to hang alongside a seaport view by

Claude, probably the work that he had once wept before when it was in Angerstein's collection.

It is not surprising that Turner called *Dido building Carthage* his 'chef d'oeuvre' or that he held it in such high esteem. He had long wanted to paint a seaport scene worthy of comparison with Claude, and with *Dido* he succeeded. Yet the painting also probably summarized everything he was trying so hard and so opaquely to articulate in the perspective lectures. With its mastery of perspective, its superb exploration of light, shade and reflections, and its total congruence between lighting, pictorial structure and content, it is certainly far more eloquent than Turner's tortuous verbal discourses.

At the Academy two years later Turner exhibited the companion painting to *Dido building Carthage*, namely *The Decline of the Carthaginian Empire*, while in the intervening 1816 show he displayed two complementary pictures of a Greek temple. In one work he portrayed the building as it appeared in contemporary eyes, and thus under Turkish subjugation, and in the other he showed it as it had perhaps looked in all its glory in ancient times, and how it might again look if Greece were free. These paintings were Turner's most open statements of his libertarianism to date.

Turner's sympathy with contemporary demands for political and religious freedom first seems to have found expression around 1800 in works alluding to contemporary struggles for liberty in Britain and abroad. During this period he was hoping to gain election as an Academician and many of the leading Royal Academicians, such as Barry, Fuseli and Smirke, were known to hold libertarian opinions. Around that time some of Turner's future patrons, such as Walter Fawkes, even held republican convictions, and undoubtedly Turner was later sympathetic to Fawkes's radicalism. The painter is known to have read banned radical political literature in the early

1820s, and he went on subtly expressing his libertarian views during that decade and the early 1830s as the Greeks struggled for their freedom and the demands for parliamentary reform in Britain quickened. Between 1829 and 1833 he subtly alluded to such struggles in a number of works, and in one design — a watercolour of a Parliamentary election in Northampton — he even made his sympathies with the reform of Parliament quite plain, for the drawing shows the election of Lord Althorp, the Chancellor of the Exchequer in the reformist administration of Lord Grey. Naturally, Turner also celebrated the attainment of Greek freedom in 1830, in a watercolour of a fountain on the island of Chios that is discussed below. The artist's identification with libertarianism was entirely understandable, given his lowly origins.

Turner continued touring during these years. In 1811, 1813 and 1814 he visited the West Country in order to obtain material for the 'Southern Coast' series and other engraving schemes, and in 1813 he had a particularly enjoyable time in Plymouth where he was much fêted locally, treated his friends to picnics, took boat rides in stormy weather (which he enjoyed enormously, having good sea-legs), and even painted in oils in the open air. This was an unusual practice for Turner, although he set no artistic store on his oil sketches and never exhibited them.

In 1816 Turner made an extensive tour of the north of England to gather subjects for watercolours intended for engraving in the 'History of Richmondshire' scheme, a survey of the area around Richmond in Yorkshire and Lonsdale in Lancashire. Originally Turner was to have made 120 watercolours for the 'Richmondshire' project, and to have been paid the huge sum of 3000 guineas for those drawings, but unfortunately the venture petered out owing to lack of public enthusiasm, and Turner made only some 21 of the designs.

In 1817 the painter revisited the Continent, stopping off at the scene of the recent battle of Waterloo before touring the Rhineland and visiting Amsterdam. Impressive paintings of Waterloo and of the river Maas at Dordrecht were exhibited at the Royal Academy the following year. *The Field of Waterloo* is a picture stylistically influenced by Rembrandt, and it is also surprisingly modern in its treatment of its subject, for Turner eschewed vainglory in the work and instead took a very pessimistic, anti-war position. The view of Dordrecht is an idyllic river scene in which Turner paid homage to one of his favourite Dutch painters, Aelbert Cuyp. The work was bought by Walter Fawkes who installed it over the fireplace at Farnley Hall as the centrepiece of his collection. In 1817 Fawkes had also bought the complete set of 51 watercolours that Turner had made earlier that year in the Rhineland, and in 1819 he put his large collection of watercolours by Turner on display in his London house, an exhibition that was opened to the public. For the catalogue Fawkes wrote an impressive dedication to Turner, stating that he was never able to look at the artist's works 'without intensely feeling the delight I have experienced, during the greater part of my life, from the exercise of your talent and the pleasure of your society.'

In 1819 Turner at long last visited Italy, although he had already made a number of superb watercolours of Italian scenery that he had developed from sketches by others (one of them is reproduced on the cover of this book). On his tour Turner visited Milan, Venice, Rome, Naples, Sorrento and Paestum, before turning northwards. He probably spent Christmas in Florence and began his return journey in late January 1820, once more crossing the Mont Cenis pass where his coach overturned during a snowstorm. He arrived back in London loaded down with some 2000 sketches and studies, and immediately started one of his largest paintings for display at

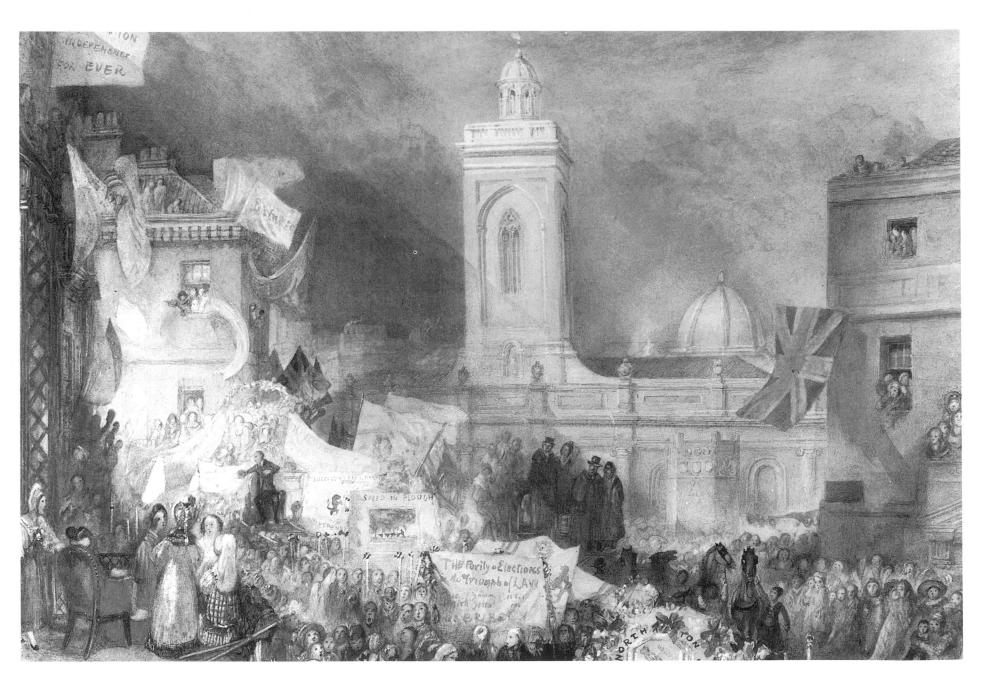

Northampton, Northamptonshire, *Winter 1830–31.*

the 1820 Royal Academy exhibition, a view from the loggia of the Vatican, with Raphael in the foreground. The three hundredth anniversary of Raphael's death fell in 1820, and Turner therefore aptly celebrated his immortality.

Although Turner was increasingly busy making small watercolours for the engravers during the 1820s (such as the jewel-like drawing of *Portsmouth* discussed below), perhaps the most impressive achievements of the first half of the decade were the large and superbly wrought watercolours made for the 'Marine Views' scheme (of which two examples are reproduced below), and the paintings of *The Bay of Baiæ, with Apollo and the Sybil*, shown at the Academy in 1823, and of *The Battle of Trafalgar* created between 1822 and 1824 to hang in St James's Palace. In *The Bay of Baiæ* Turner again made clear his continuing sense of irony, for in the work the Cumaean Sibyl begs Apollo for endless life, and has her wish granted, but forgets to request the eternal good looks to accompany it; the beauty of the surrounding landscape underlines the pathetic and wholly ironical failure of human aspirations by contrast, while the ruined buildings in the background anticipate and parallel the forthcoming ruin of the Sibyl herself. *The Battle of Trafalgar* was the largest picture Turner ever painted and it resulted from the only Royal commission he was to receive, but it was not liked and was soon shunted off to hang in the Royal Naval Hospital at Greenwich.

In 1824 Turner unknowingly visited Farnley Hall for the last time, for in October 1825 Walter Fawkes died and the painter refused to visit the house ever again, so imbued was it with precious memories for him. Turner was clearly shattered by Fawkes's death, and he had good reason to be, for the Yorkshireman was only six years older than he was himself. Early in 1827 Turner wrote to a friend:

Alas! my good Auld lang sine is gone . . . and I must follow; indeed, I feel as you say, near a million times the brink of eternity, with me daddy only steps in between as it were . . .

That brink moved appreciably closer in September 1829 when Turner's father died, leaving the painter utterly disconsolate; as a friend remarked, 'Turner never appeared the same man after his father's death; his family was broken up.' He and his father had always been especially close, doubtless because of their mutual reliance upon each other during the illness of the painter's mother. The senior William Turner had served for many years as his son's factotum, and he both stretched his offspring's canvases and varnished them when they were completed, leading Turner to joke that his father both started and finished his pictures for him. That Turner did feel nearer 'the brink of eternity' after his father's death is made clear by the fact that the painter drew up the first draft of his will less than ten days after the old man's demise.

The deaths of Fawkes and Turner's father were joined by other losses at this time, most notably that of Sir Thomas Lawrence early in 1830. Turner commemorated Lawrence's funeral in an impressive watercolour he exhibited at the Royal Academy the following summer, the last watercolour he ever displayed there. And because Turner refused ever to visit Farnley again, after 1826 he took to regularly staying at another 'home from home' owned by one of his patrons, namely Petworth House in Sussex, the country seat of George Wyndham, the third Earl of Egremont. The earl was a collector of enormous taste and vigour, and he had bought his first painting from Turner early in the century; by the time of his death he owned nineteen of Turner's oil paintings. At Petworth Turner was free to come and go at his leisure, although the age difference between the artist and his patron (the

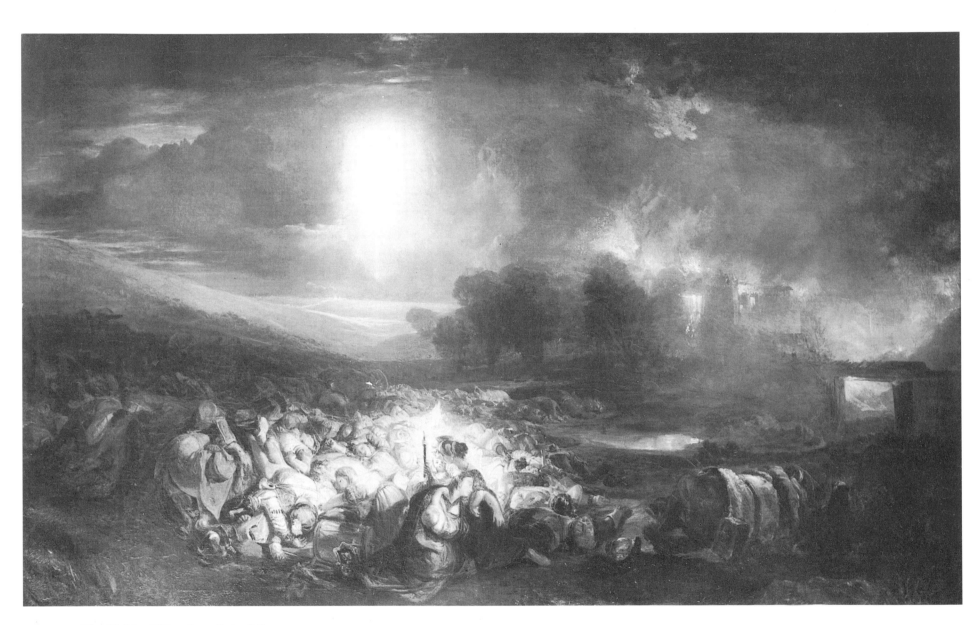

The Field of Waterloo, *R.A. 1818*.

earl was seventy-five when the fifty-one-year-old painter began regularly revisiting the house in 1826) meant that the two men were never as close as Turner and Walter Fawkes had been. After Lord Egremont died in 1837 Turner shunned Petworth, just as he shunned Farnley Hall, and for the same reason: death shut certain doors in his life.

In 1825 Turner embarked upon yet another ambitious set of watercolours destined for engraving, the series entitled 'Picturesque Views in England and Wales', a group of drawings that quite rightly has been called 'the central document of his art'. Like the 'Richmondshire' series, it was to have comprised 120 drawings, and the painter created about 100 watercolours for the project before public indifference led to its cancellation in 1838. In 1829, and again in 1833, he exhibited large groups of the 'England and Wales' watercolours and other designs; the later display must have looked especially dazzling, for it consisted of some 67 watercolours made for the series, in which every aspect of British scenery and of Turner's unrivalled mastery of the art of watercolour was evident. And throughout the 1820s and '30s the painter was frantically busy producing marvellous watercolours for a host of other engraving projects as well, including topographical surveys of the ports, rivers and east coast of England, the rivers of France (part of a scheme to survey the rivers of Europe that never got further than explorations of the Seine and Loire), and books such as the prose works of Sir Walter Scott and one treating of the landscapes of the Bible, as well as collections of the poetry of Scott, Byron, Rogers and Campbell. Well might Turner have complained, as he did in the mid-1820s, that there was 'no holiday ever for me'.

Given the pressures Turner faced in producing large numbers of watercolours for the engraver, he had of necessity evolved a production-line method for making such drawings. Two accounts of this technique have come down to us from the same witness:

There were four drawing boards, each of which had a handle screwed to the back. Turner, after sketching the subject in a fluent manner, grasped the handle and plunged the whole drawing into a pail of water by his side. Then quickly he washed in the principal hues that he required, flowing tint into tint, until this stage of the work was complete. Leaving this drawing to dry, he took a second board and repeated the operation. By the time the fourth drawing was laid in, the first would be ready for the finishing touches.

. . . [Turner] stretched the paper on boards and after plunging them into water, he dropped the colours onto the paper while it was wet, making *marblings* and gradations throughout the work. His completing process was marvellously rapid, for he indicated his masses and incidents, took out half-lights, scraped out highlights and dragged, hatched and stippled until the design was finished. This swiftness, grounded on the scale practice in early life, enabled Turner to preserve the purity and luminosity of his work, and to paint at a prodigiously rapid rate.

That the artist could maintain his inventiveness at such a 'rapid rate' and under the intense pressures put upon him by the engravers is certainly a mark of his genius.

In August 1828 Turner again visited Italy. He stayed principally in Rome where he painted and then exhibited his works publicly in a show that attracted over 1000 visitors, who were mostly mystified by what they saw. On his return journey over the alps in January 1829 Turner's coach was again overturned in the snow (as it had been in 1820), and he recorded the experience in a watercolour that he exhibited in the 1829 Academy Exhibition, a drawing in which we see the painter himself wearing a top

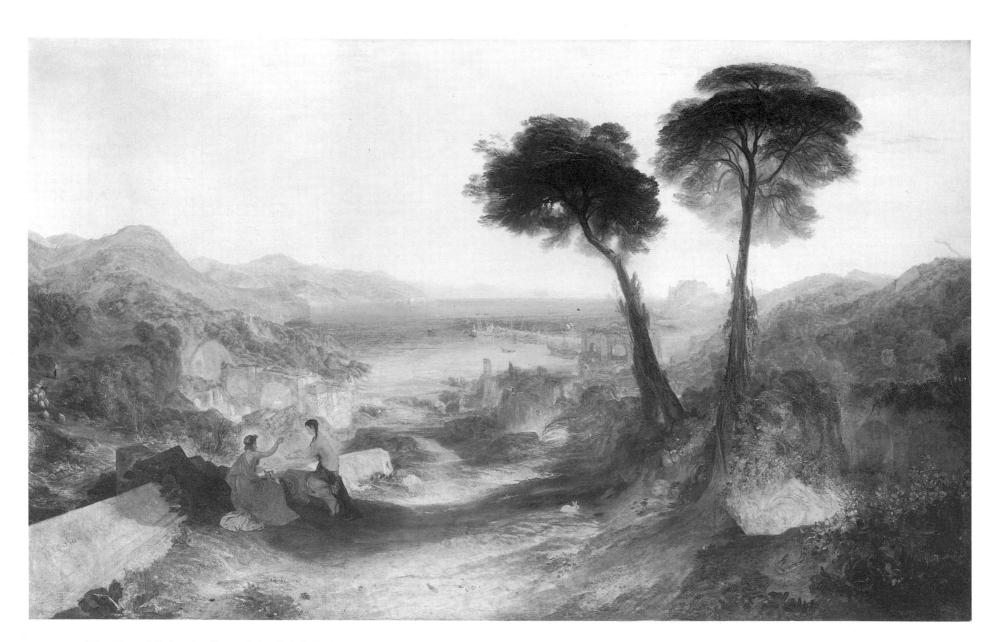

The Bay of Baiæ: Apollo and the Sybil, *R.A. 1823*.

hat and sitting in the foreground.

Another work that Turner displayed at the Academy in 1829 was the superb *Ulysses deriding Polyphemus*, in connection with which *The Times* said that 'no other artist living . . . can exercise anything like the magic power which Turner wields with such ease.' John Ruskin later called *Ulysses deriding Polyphemus* 'the *central picture* in Turner's career', and in colouristic terms at least one can see why he did so, for by now the artist was achieving an idealism of colour that was entirely commensurate with the ideality of forms he had mastered earlier. This idealism was based upon the use of the three primary colours, yellow, red and blue, and thus addressed the fundamentals of painterly colour itself.

Turner's interest in the theory of colour had been stimulated by his investigation of the science of optics undertaken in connection with the perspective lectures, and in 1818 he introduced the subject of colour into those talks that were ostensibly about spatial and pictorial organization. A subtle change took place in Turner's colour around that time also, and it may have been

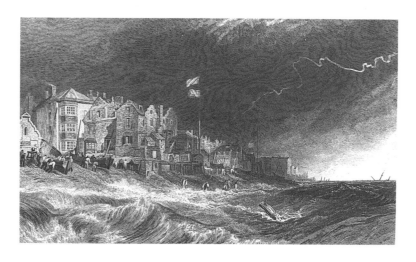

W. Radclyffe after J.M.W. Turner, Deal, Kent, *engraving for the 'Picturesque Views on the Southern Coast' series, 1826.*

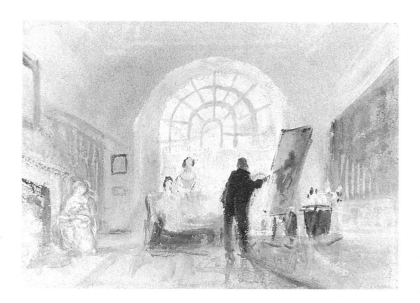

The Artist and his Admirers, *c. 1827.*

connected to his analysis of colour theory. Thereafter a greater reliance upon the primaries and a more intense luminosity becomes apparent, and certainly the change in Turner's colour was recognized at the time, for in 1823 an encyclopedia published in Edinburgh stated that Turner's 'genius seems to tremble on the verge of some new discovery in colour'. By the end of the 1820s, when *Ulysses deriding Polyphemus* appeared, such a 'discovery' had been thoroughly consolidated, and Turner was habitually creating ranges of colour that have never been matched by any other painter, let alone surpassed.

In the hanging of the 1831 Royal Academy show Turner came into conflict with John Constable. The two painters had known each other since 1813 when Constable had sat next to Turner at an Academy dinner, after which he wrote to his fiancée, 'I was a good deal entertained with Turner. I always expected to find him what I did — he is uncouth but has a wonderful range of mind.' And Constable had a very high regard for Turner's works, writing of his pictures in the 1828 exhibition that 'Turner has some golden visions, glorious and beautiful. They are only visions, but still they are art, and one could live and die with such pictures.' But in 1831 Constable was on the Academy hanging committee and he had Turner's painting of *Caligula's Palace and Bridge* replaced on the wall by one of his own works, *Salisbury Cathedral from the Meadows*. The painter David Roberts was present at a meeting of the two men soon afterwards, and he recorded what happened in his rather ungrammatical and ill-spelt prose:

> Constable a conceited egotistic person . . . was loud in describing to all the severe duties he had undergone in the hanging the Exhibition. According to his own account nothing could exceed his distineredness [*sic*] or his anxiety to discharge that Sacred Duty. Most unfortunately for him a Picture of Turners had been displaced after the arraingment of the room in which it was placed . . . Turner opened upon him like a ferret; it was evident to all present that Turner detested him; all present were puzzled what to do or say to stop this. Constable wriggled, twisted & made it appear or wished to make it appear that in his removal of the Picture he was only studying the best light or the best arraingment for Turner. The latter coming back invariably to the charge, yess, but why put your own there? — I must say that Constable looked to me and I believe to every one else, like a detected criminal, and I must add Turner slew him without remorse. But as he had brought it upon himself few if any pitied him.

However, Turner had his revenge in the Royal Academy the following year; as C.R. Leslie noted:

> In 1832, when Constable exhibited his '*Opening of Waterloo Bridge*', it was placed in . . . one of the small rooms at Somerset House. A sea-piece, by Turner, was next to it — a grey picture, beautiful and true, but with no positive colour in any part of it. Constable's 'Water-

loo' seemed as if painted with liquid gold and silver, and Turner came several times into the room while he was heightening with vermilion and lake the decorations and flags of the city barges. Turner stood behind him looking from the 'Waterloo' to his own picture, and at last brought his palette from the great room where he was touching another picture, and putting a daub of red lead, somewhat bigger than a shilling, on his grey sea, went away without saying a word. The intensity of the red lead, made more vivid by the coolness of his picture, caused even the vermilion and lake of Constable to look weak. I came into the room just as Turner left it. 'He has been here,' said Constable, 'and fired a gun.' . . . The great man did not come again into the room for a day and a half; and then, in the last moments that were allowed for painting, he glazed the scarlet seal he had put on his picture, and shaped it into a buoy.

Turner liked playing these kinds of visual games on the Academy walls, where pictures were hung frame to frame, but he did not always win them. His great friend, George Jones, recalled that in the 1833 Exhibition:

> *The View of Venice with Canaletti painting* [by Turner] hung next to a picture of mine which had a very blue sky. [Turner] joked with me about it and threatened that if I did not alter it he would put it down by bright colour, which he was soon able to do by adding blue to his own . . . and then went to work on some other picture. I enjoyed the joke and resolved to imitate it, and introduced a great deal more white into my sky, which made his look much too blue. The ensuing day, he saw what I had done, laughed heartily, slapped my back and said I might enjoy the victory.

Turner also demonstrated his virtuosity in public during the 1830s, sending to Royal Academy and British Institution exhibitions rough underpaintings that he worked up

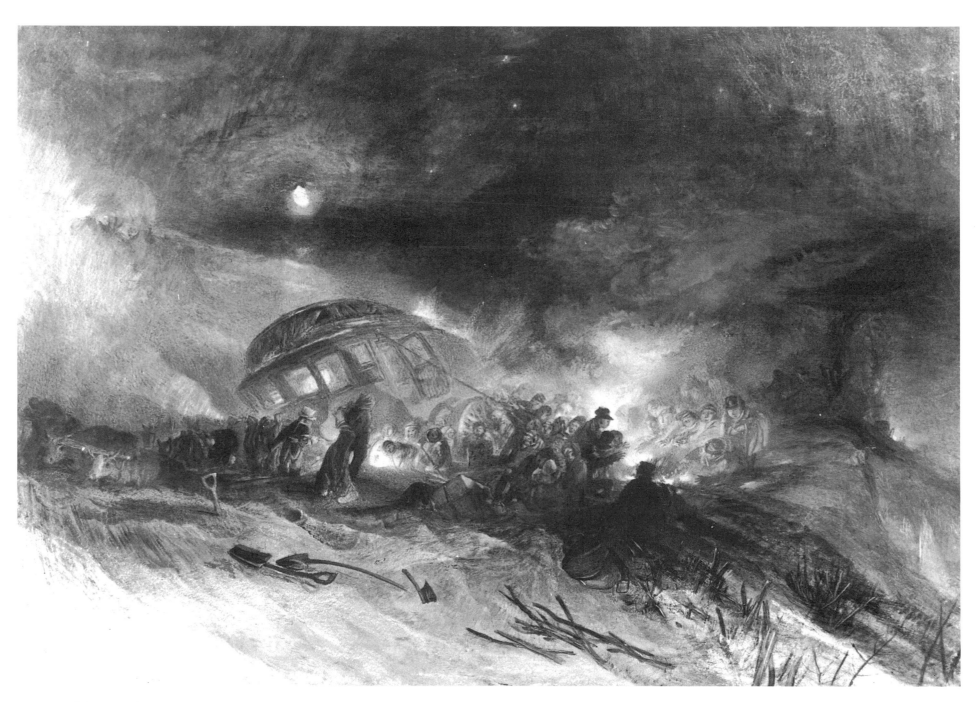

Messieurs les voyageurs on their return from Italy (par le diligence)
in a snow drift on Mount Tarrar — 22nd of January, 1829, *R.A. 1829.*

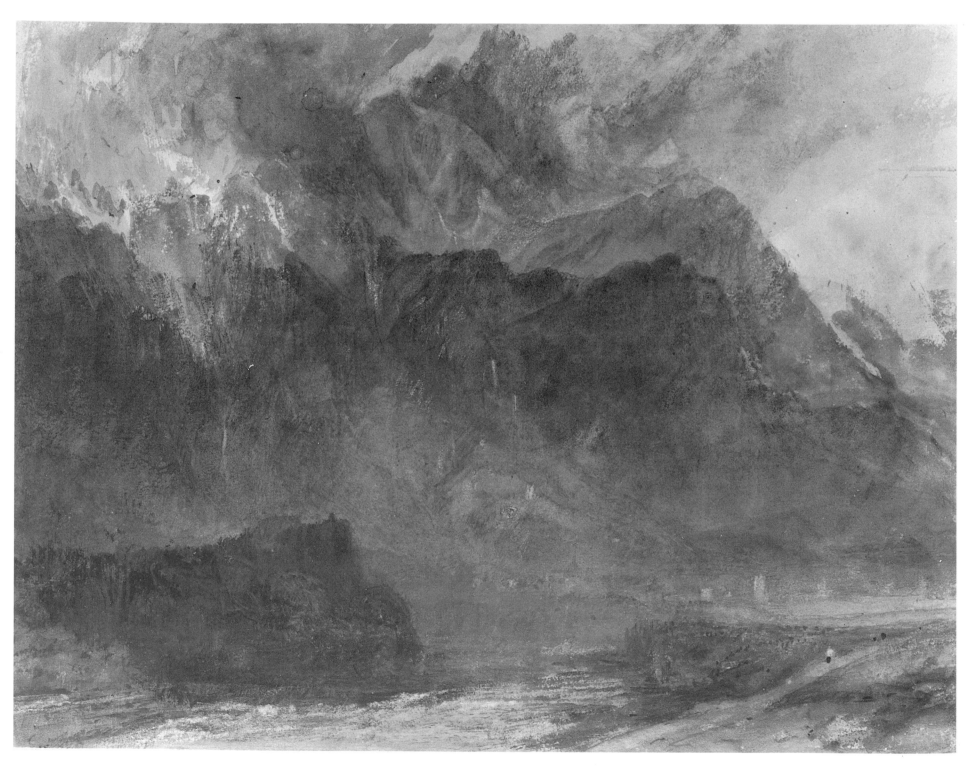

A scene in the Val d'Aosta, *c. 1836*.

to a state of completion during the days permitted for varnishing pictures. Perhaps the most spectacular recorded instance of this practice occurred on the walls of the British Institution in 1835 when Turner almost entirely painted *The Burning of the Houses of Lords and Commons* (a picture that is analysed on p. 109) in one day. He had begun work at first light and he painted all day, surrounded by a circle of admirers and without once stepping back to gauge the visual effect of his labours. Finally the picture was completed:

> Turner gathered his tools together, put them into and shut up the box, and then, with his face still turned to the wall, and at the same distance from it, went sidelong off, without speaking a word to anybody, and when he came to the staircase, in the centre of the room, hurried down as fast as he could. All looked with a half wondering smile, and Maclise, who stood near, remarked, 'There, that's masterly, he does not stop to look at his work; he *knows* it is done, and he is off.'

It has plausibly been suggested that Turner was led to demonstrate such virtuosic insouciance by the example of the violinist Paganini, who had taken London by storm in the early 1830s.

As in previous decades, during the 1830s Turner usually made annual tours in order to gain material for new works. An especially important trip took place in 1833, for in that year, perhaps inspired by a work by Clarkson Stanfield, Turner had exhibited a picture of Venice (the one he heightened with blue in competition with George Jones), and after it went on display he took the opportunity to revisit Venice as the final destination on a grand tour of Europe which began in Copenhagen and took in Berlin, Dresden, Prague, Vienna, Salzburg, Innsbruck and Verona. It seems likely that a secondary purpose of this tour was to examine some of the leading Continental art collections and museums in order to advise the committee then drawing up plans in London for the new National Gallery and Royal Academy building on the Trafalgar Square site. From 1833 onwards Venice increasingly came to dominate Turner's Italian subject-matter.

After 1833 a new companion entered the painter's life. Turner had continued to visit Margate over the years, and latterly he had taken to staying with a Mrs Sophia Caroline Booth and her husband, who died in 1833. Shortly afterwards he embarked upon a physical relationship with the widow, and eventually, in the 1840s, she moved up to London to live with Turner in a cottage that she purchased in Chelsea. David Roberts talked to Sophia Booth shortly after Turner died, and later recorded (in his imperfect prose):

> . . . for about 18 years . . . they lived together as husband & wife, under the name of Mr & Mrs Booth . . . . But the most extraordinary part of her narative is that, with the exception of the 1st year he never contributed one Shilling towards their mutual support!!! — But for 18 years she provided solely for their maintenance & living but purchased the cottage at Chelsea from money she had previously saved or inherited . . . Turner refusing to give a farthing towards it . . . She assures me that the only money She has belonging to him during this long term of years was three half crowns She found in his pocket after death, black, She says with being so long in his pocket & which she keeps as a souvenir . . .

Early on in life Turner had earned a reputation as a miser, and doubtless he had initially watched every penny because as a child he had witnessed the effects of poverty in the slum-infested Covent Garden area of London. Yet even when he became wealthy he maintained his penny-pinching habits, although after he first drew up his will in 1829 it is possible to discern some noble motive behind

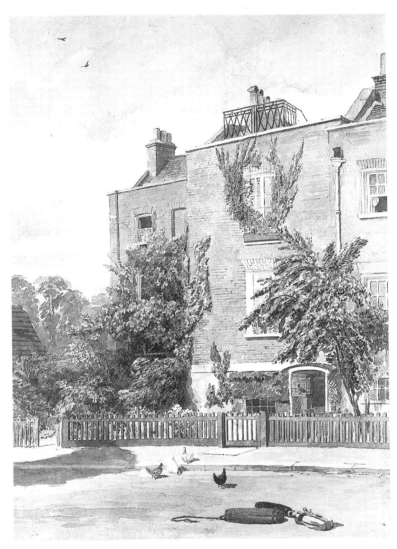

J.W. Archer, House of J.M.W. Turner at Chelsea, *1852*.

when they were auctioned off and then leaving them to rot in his house in Queen Anne Street. Moreover, although by the late 1840s Turner had begun to form his final wish that all his paintings should go to the National Gallery (a desire that he formulated in final codicils to his will in 1848 and 1849), nonetheless he did little to ensure that they were maintained in good condition. Yet despite the fear of death — an apprehensiveness that was unleavened by any belief in an afterlife — and the eccentric behaviour it led to, the artist did not let those anxieties and eccentricities darken his work. Instead his late paintings and drawings became ever more beautiful as their creator used them to ward off all the terrors of dying and to bring the idealism of a lifetime to a triumphant apotheosis.

In 1841, and for the following three summers, Turner returned to Switzerland. Four sets of watercolours resulted from those trips, and they are among the painter's very greatest creations, for in the immensity, beauty and solitude of the alps he clearly found some solace for his fears of dying. In the final set especially, drawings that were possibly made between 1846 and 1850, we can apprehend a continuous pulse running behind and through the outlines of discrete objects; the visible universe becomes filled with a primal sense of energy. These characteristics are equally evident in a group of oil paintings made after about 1843 from the old 'Liber Studiorum' images, works in which light, colour and energy are all intensified to the utmost degree, dissolving forms in the process. These paintings do not celebrate merely the physical world: their pulsating energies, intensities of light and dissolutions of form are clearly expressions of something beyond the physical. Given Turner's lifelong attraction to academic idealism, at whose core lay a Platonic metaphysical system that the painter had accepted at an early age, there can be absolutely no doubt

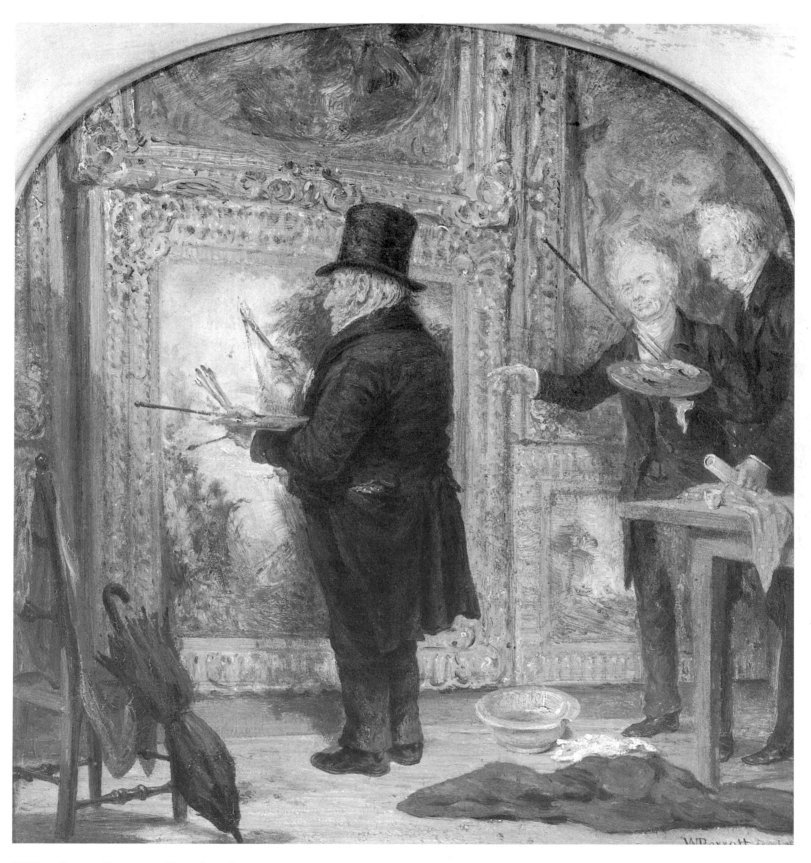

William Parrott, Turner on Varnishing Day, *c. 1846*.

that in his late, radiant images the artist was projecting an ideal reality, one corresponding to the world of the Ideas delineated by Plato. And there is no inconsistency between Turner's lifelong identification with such a metaphysical system and his supposed statement that 'The Sun is God', for the brilliant light in these late paintings is far more than simply the hedonistic sunshine later beloved of the French Impressionists. Instead we are looking at Turner's deity, the essence and fount of creation, the godhead itself, its energies running through everything.

In 1845 the painter took the chair of President of the Royal Academy for some weeks when the actual President, Sir Martin Archer Shee, was too ill to carry out his duties. And also in that same year he made the last of his sketching tours, this time to northern France, where he visited King Louis Philippe, an old friend from the days when they both lived in Twickenham. But Turner's health began to break down in 1845, and by the end of the following year it had become very bad, not being helped by the fact that he was losing all his teeth; in his final years he had to gain sustenance from sucking his food. He continued to show a few works every year at the Academy (although not in 1848, the first time since 1824 he had not exhibited), but gradually he began to lose the physical control necessary for painting. In 1850, however, he summoned forth his last vestiges of strength to display four pictures at the Royal Academy, all treatments of the Dido and Aeneas theme. The subject may have had a personal allegorical significance, for Turner's commitment to his art paralleled Aeneas's devotion to duty, a commitment that had led the Trojan prince to abandon Queen Dido in order to sail to Italy and found Rome. Like Aeneas, Turner had also forsworn an easy life, the enjoyment of wealth and the delights of the senses for a higher calling, while Queen Dido stood for everything he

had renounced.

After displaying these last four works at the Royal Academy in the late spring of 1850 it appears that Turner was too feeble physically to paint any more and he awaited death over the following eighteen months rather apprehensively and sadly. Occasionally he would be helped onto the flat roof of the Chelsea house to watch the sun rise over the low pastures of Battersea across the river (what he called the 'Dutch view'), or see it set behind the hills to the west (the 'English view'), but that was all. The rest was silence.

Turner died on 19 December 1851. In addition to nearly two thousand paintings and watercolours in private hands, he left an immense body of work in the Queen Anne Street and Chelsea studios — some 282 finished

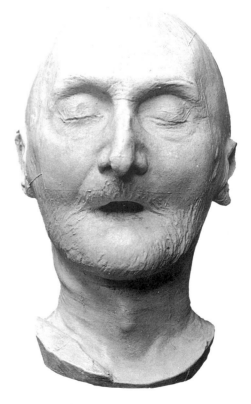

Turner's death mask.

and unfinished oil paintings and 19,049 drawings and sketches in watercolour, pencil and other media (in addition to tens of thousands of prints, which were sold off in 1874). The estate was valued at £140,000, a sum whose exact modern value is incalculable but which might conservatively be approximated if we multiply it by a hundred. The will contained two main provisions: that a gallery should be built to house Turner's works and that the charitable foundation known as 'Turner's Gift' should be created. Unfortunately, however, the will was contested by Turner's relatives and overthrown on a legal technicality, the relatives getting the money and the nation the pictures, although until 1987 no gallery was built, and only then did it come into being through private largesse and largely as a result of pressure from an action group, the Turner Society.

The triumph of private greed over the realization of 'Turner's Gift' was extremely ironic, given that the painter had been so selfless in accruing wealth for the purpose of creating his charitable foundation. Eventually, of course, the Welfare State took over the care of old, impoverished artists, so that the failure of the charity to come into being did not matter all that much. But ultimately Turner's supreme gift was his art, and that legacy lives on in a body of work that may have been equalled in size and quality, but which has never been surpassed for its beauty, power and insight into the nature of the human condition, and the conditions in which we live.

ERIC SHANES
LONDON, DECEMBER 1989

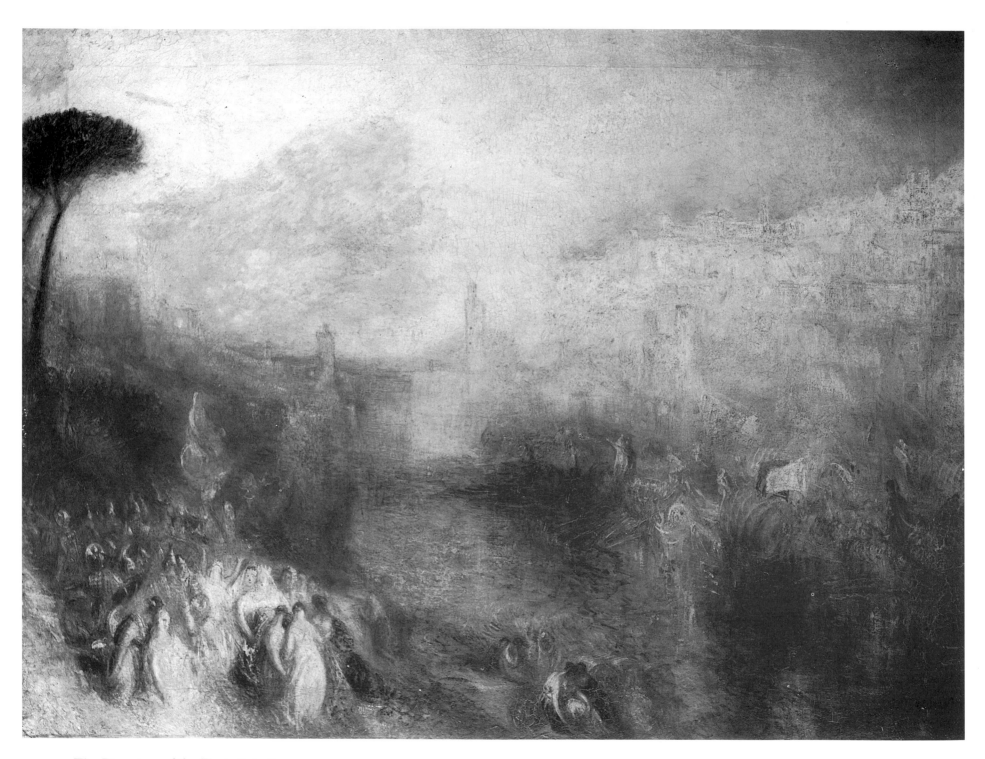

The Departure of the Fleet, *R.A. 1850.*

THE PLATES

The Archbishop's Palace, Lambeth, 1790

26.3 × 37.8 cm. Indianapolis Museum of Art

This watercolour was Turner's first exhibited work, displayed at the Royal Academy in 1790 when he was just fifteen years old. It demonstrates great self-assurance for one so young, especially in projecting a group of buildings that are aligned at different angles to one another. Stylistically the work shows the influence of Thomas Malton, Jr, to whom Turner had loosely apprenticed himself while officially studying at the Royal Academy Schools where painting was not taught. Malton's influence can especially be detected in the marked perspective of the buildings on the right, the shaping and tonal definition of the clouds, the elongation of the foreground figures, the role of those people in establishing the character of the place, and its scale. From left to right we see a boatman, with Westminster Bridge beyond; some boys playing with a hoop; a washerwoman making her way down to the Thames, presumably to do her washing in the river; a dandy and his young lady; a youth courting a girl in the window of a wineshop; and a covered gig.

The control of light is already masterly, with the hidden, early morning sun casting long, soft shadows, exactly the kind of effect that is apparent soon after dawn when the light is still hazy with river mist. It seems entirely characteristic that the young Turner looked *towards* the light, which is not always the easiest effect to bring off convincingly, even for very experienced artists. And in the shadowed side of the buildings on the right we can equally perceive Turner's powers of observation, for the shadows are distributed unevenly, being affected by stainings on the walls themselves and by reflections off the old Lambeth Road in front of them. Turner would later devote one of his annual perspective lectures at the Royal Academy to the study of reflections, and we can detect his interest in the subject even when he was only halfway through his teens.

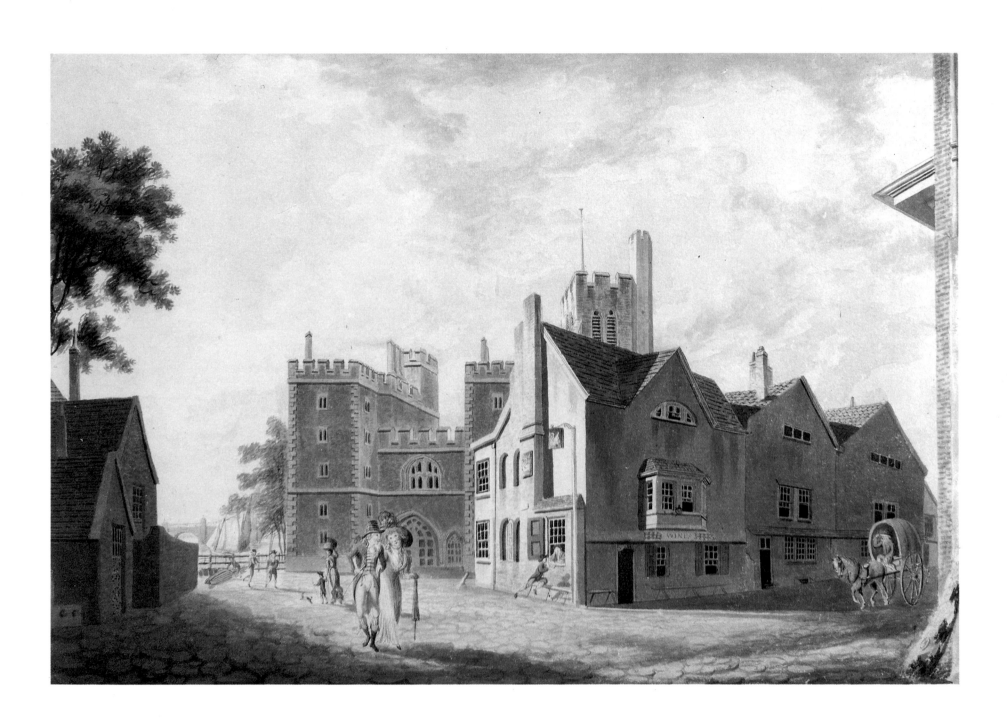

St Anselm's Chapel, with part of Thomas-à-Becket's crown, Canterbury Cathedral, 1794

51.7 × 37.4 cm. Whitworth Art Gallery, Manchester

Turner probably developed this superb watercolour from sketches made in either 1792 or 1793, and it was exhibited at the Royal Academy in 1794. We look from the south-east corner of Canterbury Cathedral towards the octagon known as the 'corona' or crown where were once enshrined the remains of the head of Saint Thomas-à-Becket, who was murdered elsewhere in the cathedral in 1170. In the later Middle Ages this part of the building had been the leading pilgrimage shrine in England, as *The Canterbury Tales* attests.

The low viewpoint displays the continuing influence of Thomas Malton, Jr, for such depressed angles were a typical Maltonian pictorial device. But the depiction of the masonry shows the influence of another leading British topographical artist, namely Michael Angelo Rooker, who was exceptionally able at portraying the varied textures of masonry with a masterly control of different tones. Rooker's influence may especially be detected on the left where each slab of masonry is tinted in a slightly different tone from its neighbours, within a governing overall tone that gradually darkens upwards. Such a control of tone would have an important long-term effect on Turner, for the minute differentiation of light and dark ultimately governed his control of colour, especially in the late works where often whole areas are saturated with a single colour, within which the narrowest tonal variations nonetheless project wide spatial differences.

This drawing makes it clear that even at nineteen Turner was already an absolute master at painting architecture. Due to its complexity, the south-east corner of Canterbury Cathedral is a very difficult structure to depict, the main bulk of the cathedral and its octagon presenting a series of differently angled facets from which buttresses and towers jut out in all directions. But Turner has not only unified all those jumbled surfaces into a coherent whole; he has also captured the multitudinous reflections, highlights and shadows that fall across them as they catch the early morning light. Moreover, equally evident is the young artist's total comprehension of the underlying dynamics of the architecture, its volumes, masses, stresses and other physical interactions. Within a short time of making this work, Turner's understanding of such dynamics would extend to the underlying constants of natural architecture as well.

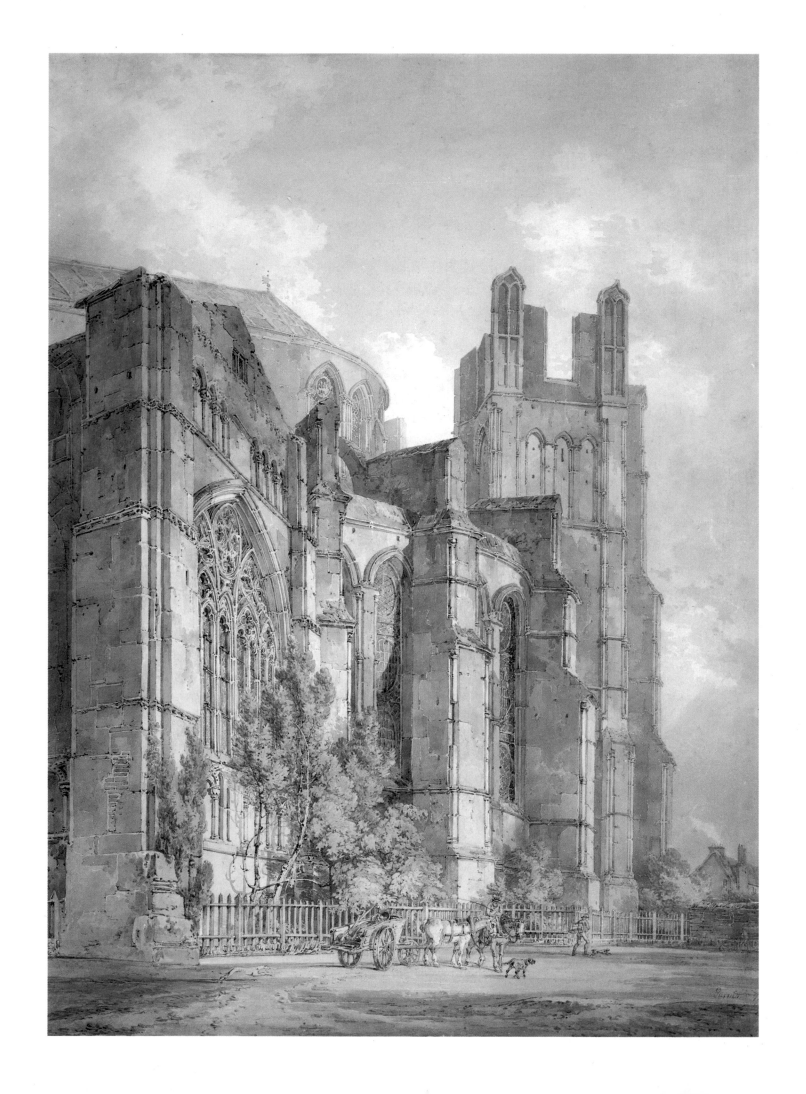

Fishermen at Sea, 1796

91.5 × 122.4 cm. Clore Gallery for the Turner Collection, London

Turner made his debut as an oil painter with this picture, in the Royal Academy Exhibition of 1796. In the work we look southwards towards the Needles, the group of rocks that extends along an east-west axis off the western end of the Isle of Wight. Yet we would not be able to see the southern coast of the Isle of Wight in the far distance if we looked from this selfsame viewpoint in reality, for it would stretch away to the left. Clearly Turner has ignored the constraints of literalism and brought Freshwater Bay and St Catherine's Point into the picture so as to intensify our understanding of the relationship of the Needles to the adjacent island, as well as to create a more interesting background. In doing so he was probably following the injunctions of Reynolds to synthesize his landscape from the best features of *several* viewpoints, thus transcending the 'Accidents of Nature'. Such an interpretation is supported by the generalized title which does not specify a particular place.

The depiction of the sea demonstrates a mastery of both particularities and generalities. The understanding of the first can be seen in the way that the turbulent waters of the Solent are contrasted with the calmer waters of the English Channel beyond, while the comprehension of universals can be witnessed in Turner's projection of the underlying swell of the sea. And artistically a number of influences are apparent here. For example, the way the sea is painted shows the influence of the French marine painter Joseph Vernet, while the night effect has been influenced by Wright of Derby's moonlight scenes, and the shaping of the clouds demonstrates the influence of Philippe Jacques de Loutherbourg. But the brilliance of lighting and the sense of bobbing movement are completely Turner's own.

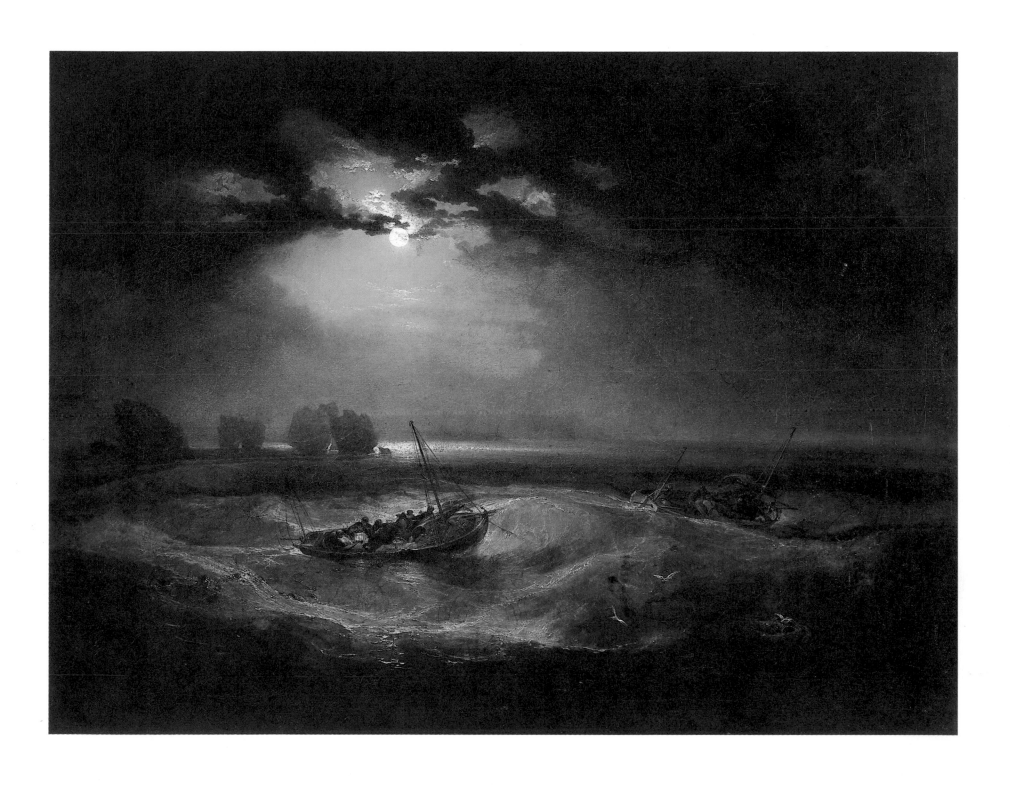

Dutch Boats in a Gale: Fishermen endeavouring to put their Fish on Board, 1801

162.5 × 222 cm. Private Collection, on loan to the National Gallery, London

Turner set the seal on his growing fame with this painting. It was commissioned by one of Britain's leading collectors, the third Duke of Bridgewater (hence the nickname of the picture, 'The Bridgewater Seapiece'), who wanted the work to hang in his gallery at Bridgewater House alongside a painting by Willem van de Velde the younger entitled *A Rising Gale*, now in the Toledo Museum of Art, Toledo, Ohio. A marked feature of the van de Velde is the marked stress that is given to a sprit or diagonal spar that supports the mainsail on a nearby Dutch fishing vessel. In 'The Bridgewater Seapiece' Turner cleverly reversed this diagonal so that although the sprit on his fishing boat is not visible, being masked by its sail, nonetheless its existence is equally evident and it enjoys an identical visual stress, albeit in the opposite direction. These opposed diagonals must have effected a strong complementary linkage between the works on the walls of Bridgewater House.

The composition is further unified by the diagonal line of approaching storm-clouds and the diagonal, rising line of shadow on the sea. In the water we can witness Turner's grasp of the fundamentals of hydrodynamic movement, the 'qualities and causes, effects and incidents' governing its motion. In the far distance may be seen a lee-shore, the bane of a sailor's life in the days of sail, when a strong wind blowing towards the shore would propel a boat landwards without any means of countering it other than anchoring and riding it out, an option that has been chosen by the distant large vessels.

The painting caused a sensation when it went on display at the Royal Academy in 1801. The President of the institution, Benjamin West, remarked that the picture was the kind of seascape that Rembrandt had wanted to paint but could not achieve (he was probably thinking of a famous Rembrandt then in England but now in the Isabella Stewart Gardner Museum in Boston, Massachusetts, showing Jesus in a small boat on the Sea of Galilee). Nor was West the only person to compare Turner to Rembrandt, for the R.A. Professor of Painting, Henry Fuseli, similarly effected the comparison and, indeed, called this work the best picture in the exhibition, remarking that its figures were 'also very clever'. He had obviously recognized the way that Turner had matched the style of the figures to the subject of the work by painting them in the manner of the Lowlands artist, David Teniers the younger, thus making them look like very salty seadogs indeed.

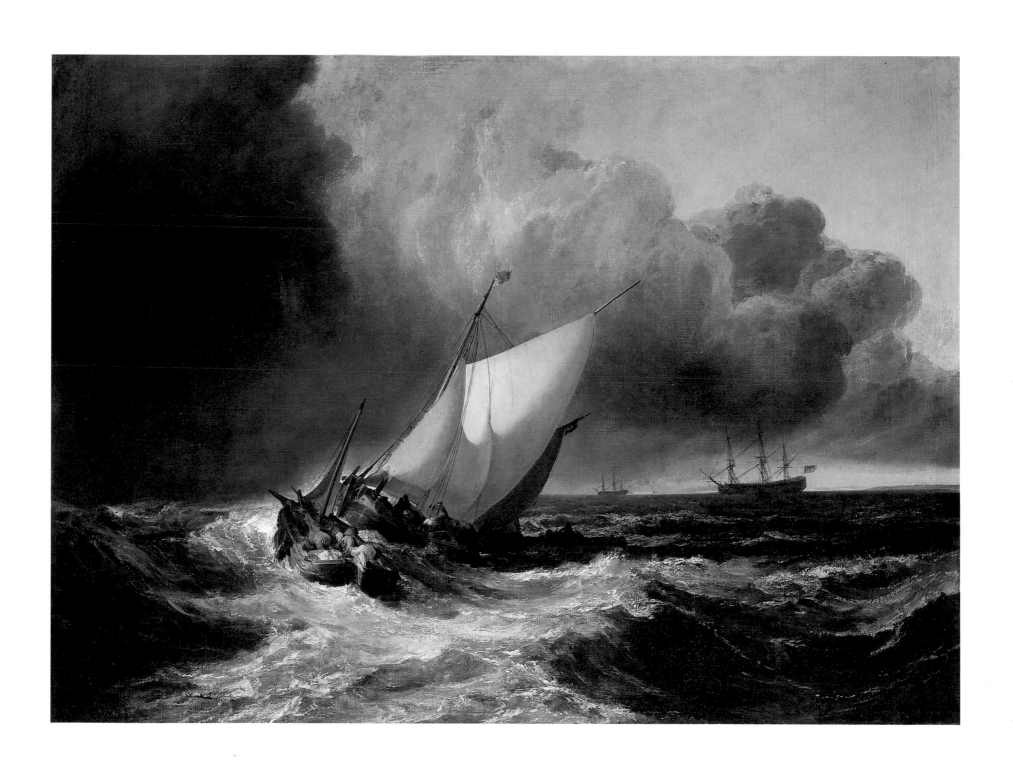

Interior of Salisbury Cathedral, looking towards the North Transept, c. 1802–1805

66 × 50.8 cm. Salisbury and South Wiltshire Museum

Here Turner made his love of architecture into the lifeblood of truly great art. Around 1797 a prominent banker, landowner, antiquarian and amateur artist, Sir Richard Colt Hoare, commissioned the painter to make ten large watercolours of Salisbury Cathedral and ten smaller drawings of buildings in and around Salisbury for use as illustrations to a history of Wiltshire he was planning. However, this work failed to materialize and so none of the designs was ever engraved. The first of the watercolours was made in 1797, but Turner never completed the commission, only finally delivering eight drawings of the cathedral for the larger set (of which this is one) and nine of the smaller designs.

In the late afternoon sunlight flooding the interior, choristers make their way toward the organ loft for Evensong. Turner's love of reflected light can be witnessed to the full here, and those reflections enrich every shadowed corner of the building, enhancing our awareness of its innate complexity and grandeur.

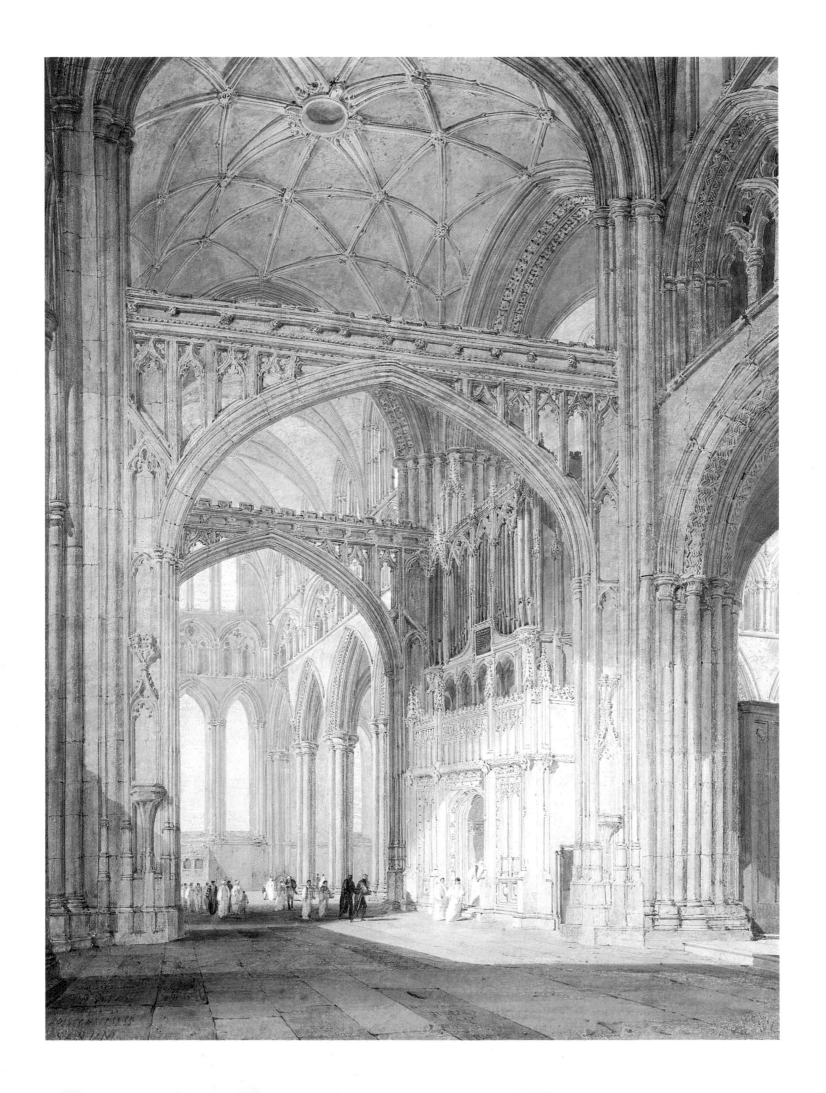

Calais Pier, with French Poissards preparing for Sea: an English Packet arriving, 1803

172 × 240 cm. National Gallery, London

As a result of the peace agreement between Britain and France in March 1802, Turner was able to visit the Continent for the first time later that year. He landed in Calais en route for Switzerland, and had to transfer from the cross-channel packet-boat to a smaller craft because the tide prevented his ferry from immediately entering harbour; according to a note in one of his sketchbooks, his small boat was 'Nearly swampt' in the process. However, what we see here is not necessarily what Turner actually witnessed at Calais in 1802.

The work was painted in the autumn, winter and spring of 1802–3 and exhibited at the Royal Academy in May 1803. During that period, and especially from 8 March 1803 onwards, all the talk in London was of the resumption of hostilities with France, and such talk may have determined Turner's imagery in this picture. To the left of centre is the English channel packet entering harbour, with the Union Jack flying from its headmast and bedraggled and presumably seasick passengers on deck (the 21-mile crossing could take up to a week, depending on the winds and tides). Just in front of the packet and taking evasive action to avoid colliding with it is one of the 'French Poissards preparing for sea' mentioned in the title, the word 'Poissard' being Turner's corruption of the word 'poissarde', meaning fish-wife. The fact that this foreign vessel is nearly involved in a collision so soon after leaving its berth is surely Turner's witty, if somewhat jingoistic comment upon the poor seamanship of the French. Equally the near-collision may allude to the fact that until recently the British and the French had also been on a collision course with one another, and had similarly averted 'collision' by agreeing to a peace. This interpretation receives support from the location of these boats immediately beneath the only peaceful area in the entire work, the glimpse of blue sky above them. If the surrounding clouds are opening then that too parallels the coming of peace; if they are closing, then they could herald the resumption of hostilities, which in fact did take place only sixteen days after this work made its public debut at the Royal Academy. Moreover, the caricatural foreground figures also seem to pander to anti-French sentiment, for they belong to the tradition of such caricatures in British art typified by Hogarth's *Calais Gate*, which Turner surely knew.

The representation of the sky seems somewhat theatrical, for the clouds are rather reminiscent of the 'flats' of stage scenery; within a couple of years Turner would instead express the 'qualities and causes' of clouds. But the sea seems entirely convincing, with its immense sense of energy, tidal flow and ideality of form. Turner's contemporaries found the definition of things rather too vague in this work, but of course that very 'indistinctness' adds to the veracity and dynamism of the image.

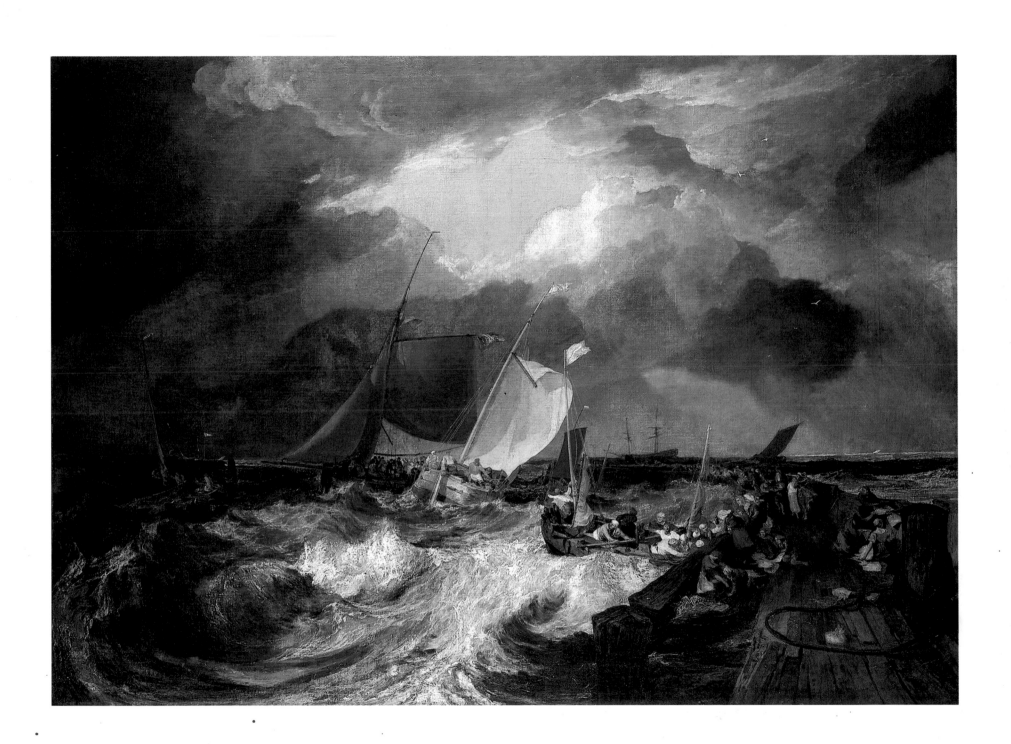

The Great Fall of the Riechenbach, in the valley of Hasle, Switzerland, 1804

102.2 × 68.9 cm. Cecil Higgins Art Gallery, Bedford

The spelling given above is Turner's own. The Reichenbach waterfall, in the Hasli valley near Meiringen, was an obvious tourist attraction for the painter to head for in 1802, and he created two highly detailed watercolours of the cascade, the other, smaller one showing it from a much nearer viewpoint and at a more oblique angle.

This is perhaps the most magnificent watercolour to have been made soon after the first Swiss tour, and it was based upon a monochromatic study dating from 1802 that is now in the National Gallery of Ireland. That the artist also thought highly of the work is demonstrated by the fact that he exhibited it over ten years after painting it, at the Royal Academy in 1815. Its upright format enhances the immense scale of the landscape, and through contrast that vastness is equally boosted by the tiny distant figures gathered around a fire on the left and the solitary goatherd clambering after strays on the hillside opposite. Making these strays so prominent was a clever psychological stratagem, for they add to our sense that disorientation is the norm in this landscape. The fundamental geological verities of the escarpment are very apparent, and at the base of the falls we can also perceive how large bodies of water cascading from a very great height give off a fine spray. In the foreground all 'the rubbish of creation' is sharply defined but its visual coherence does not diminish our sense that we are looking at nature in an especially raw state. And by making the river Reichenbach career out of the bottom of the work, Turner suggests that we are on the edge of a precipice, thus furthering the intense spatiality and drama of the scene, as well as our feeling of dislocation.

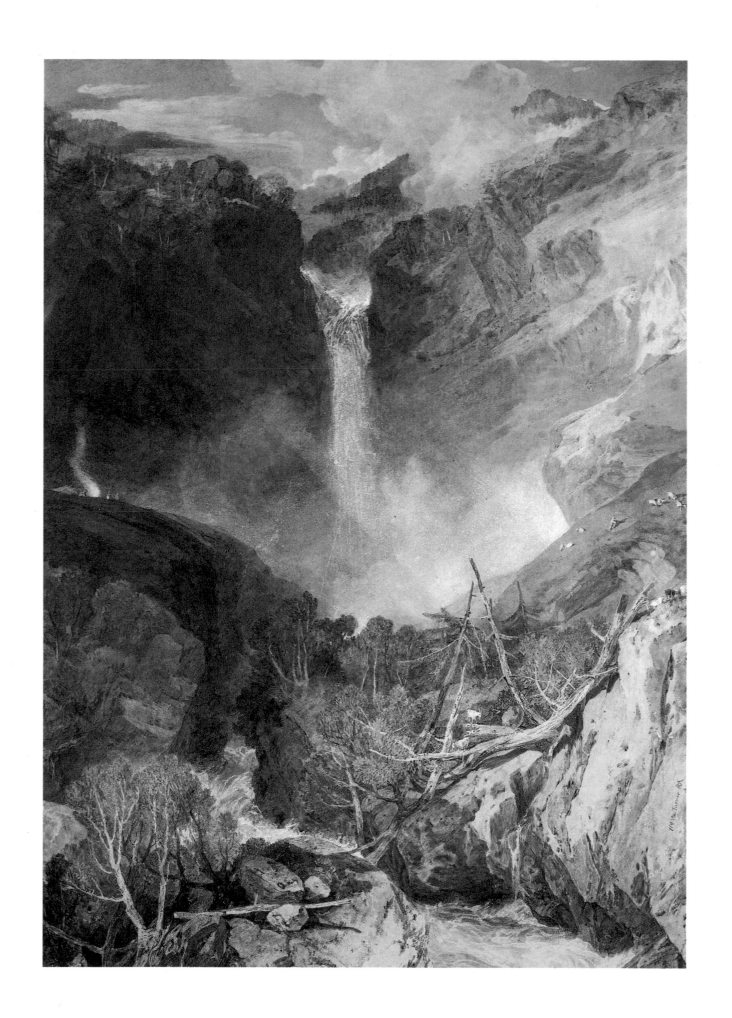

The Shipwreck, 1805

170.5 × 241.5 cm. Clore Gallery for the Turner Collection, London

Turner exhibited this ferocious seascape in his own gallery in 1805 and sold it the following year to Sir John Leicester. However, the baronet exchanged it for another painting in 1807, as he had recently lost a relative by drowning and found the subject too painful to live with.

Turner could have distributed his shipping evenly over a wide arena here but instead characteristically jumbled the major vessels together, with a capsized merchantman in the distance on the right being partially masked by a fishing boat whose crew are attempting to rescue the passengers of a lifeboat. Turner often obscured vessels in this way, and probably he did so because of his love of form: such confusions allowed him to create complex abstract shapes. On the merchantman people cling to the bowsprit rigging, tops and decks. The sea is a mass of boiling foam, in which Turner's total grasp of the verities of hydrodynamic motion and underlying energy is abundantly evident.

Given the sad fact that passenger vessels still capsize from time to time, this tragic work remains wholly relevant today. And the painting also contains a moral dimension. As in several of his earlier seascapes, including 'The Bridgewater Seapiece' and *Calais Pier*, Turner fashioned many of the figures in the style of the Flemish painter David Teniers the younger. Such gauche-looking people point up by contrast all the 'littleness of man' and the futility of human aspirations in trying to overcome the vast forces of Nature.

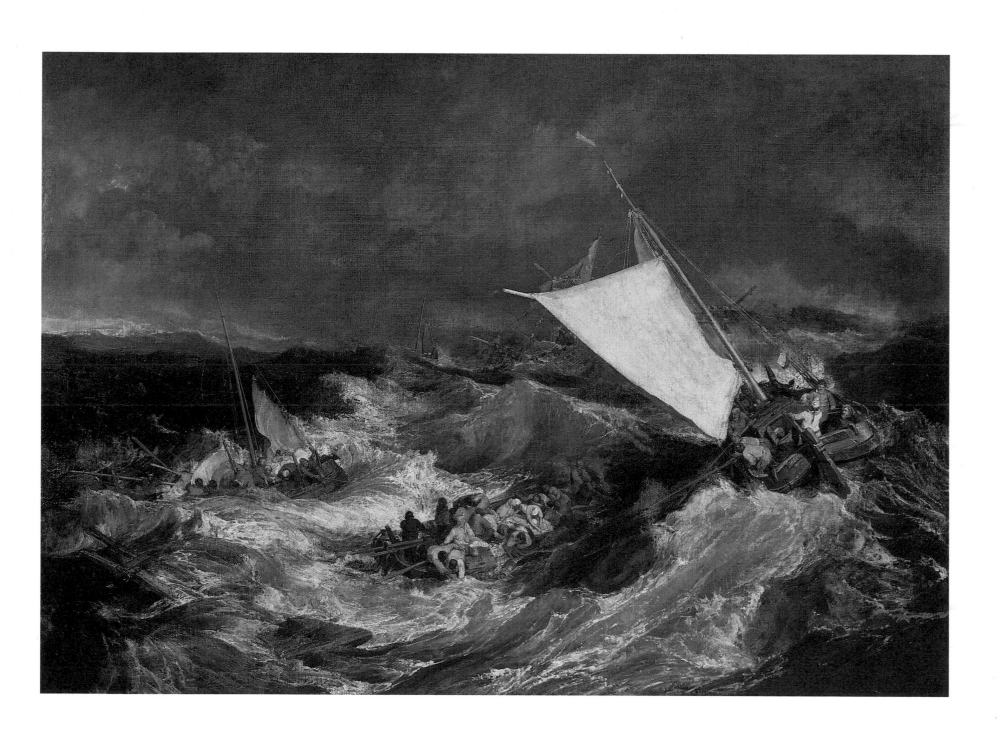

Sun rising through Vapour; Fishermen cleaning and selling Fish, 1807

134.5 × 179 cm. National Gallery, London

Turner exhibited this work at the Royal Academy in 1807, and again the following year at the British Institution. When he finally sold it to Sir John Leicester in 1818 he specified in a letter that it was a Dutch scene, but it was an entirely imaginary one, for when he painted the picture he had never been to Holland.

Again the marked influence of David Teniers the younger can be detected in the figures, although for slightly different reasons than those evident in pictures discussed above. Here the gauche figures are at extreme odds with the beauty of external nature, while equally they call forth apt Lowlands associations. The man to the right of centre standing with his hands behind his back and wearing a red cap particularly resembles a similar figure in a Teniers painting that was in an English private collection to which Turner enjoyed access when he painted this work.

The contrast between natural beauty and rough-hewn humanity is not the only antithesis here; the peacefulness of sea and sky are also subtly countered by the noisiness of mankind, with the morning gun being fired by a man-of-war in the far distance and the fishermen chattering among themselves. The depiction of the soft, hazy sunlight is especially lovely.

When Turner first drafted his will in 1829 he left two paintings to the National Gallery on condition that they hung alongside specific paintings by Claude Lorrain. These were *Dido building Carthage; or, the Rise of the Carthaginian Empire* and *The Decline of the Carthaginian Empire*, both of which are discussed below. In a second version of his will in 1831 he substituted the present painting for the decline of Carthage picture, probably because he wanted to show the Dutch side of his art rather than two exercises in the Claudian, Italianate manner. Both *Dido* and this work are sunrises (the decline of Carthage is a sunset), and maybe that factor also had something to do with the substitution, for by 1831 Turner had come to associate sunsets with death. Perhaps he preferred to hang alongside Claude in a wholly optimistic mood.

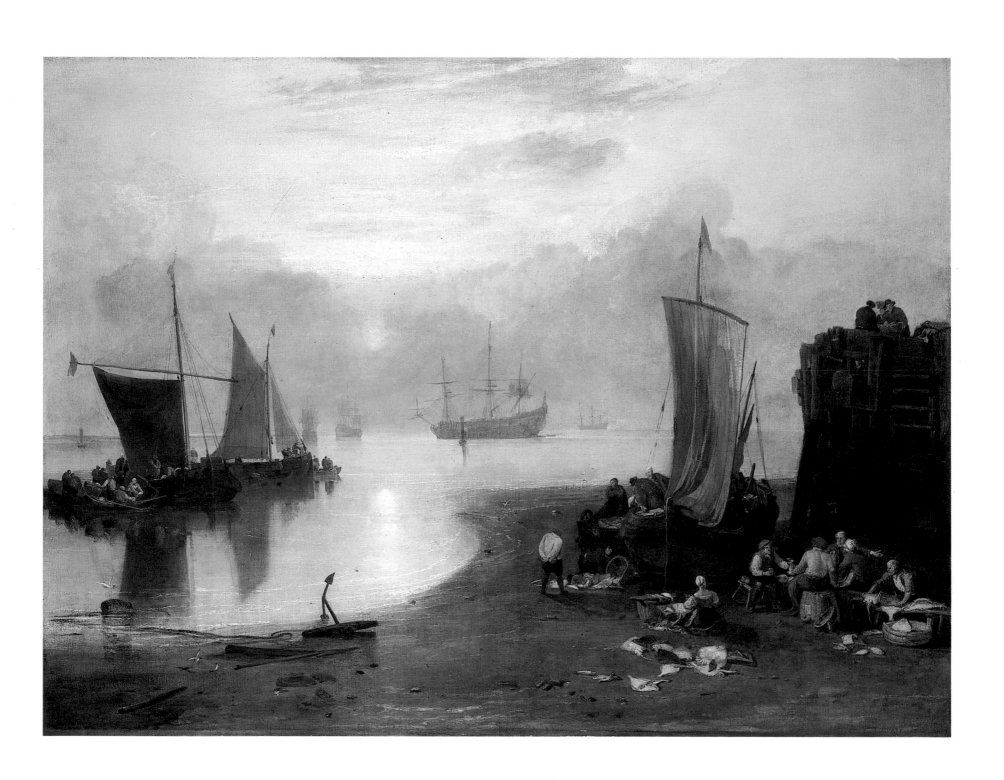

Pope's Villa at Twickenham, 1808

91.5 × 120.6 cm. Sudeley Castle, Winchcombe, Gloucestershire

This lovely painting was exhibited in Turner's gallery in 1808, from where it was bought by Sir John Leicester. The villa of Alexander Pope (1688–1744) was demolished in November 1807 by Baroness Howe who was both annoyed by the constant stream of visitors to the poet's old house and because she found it too small to accommodate her large family and busy social life. The demolition caused outrage, with Lady Howe being called the 'Queen of the Goths', but in the days before the existence of conservation orders on properties of historic interest there was nothing anyone could do to prevent it.

We know from a letter that Turner wrote in 1811 about the engraving of this picture that he intended the dead tree in the foreground to allude to a famous tree that had been planted by Alexander Pope, a tree that was believed to have been the very first weeping willow ever grown in Britain. (According to legend, Pope had been present at a soirée at Marble Hill House nearby in Twickenham when a box of books from Spain was opened and amid the packing material he spied a live twig that he subsequently planted; Turner knew this story.) The tree had been maintained by successive owners of Pope's villa until it died of natural causes in 1801, whereupon it was bought by an enterprising London jeweller who made a fortune selling pieces of it to admirers of the dead poet.

Only a very rough sketch of this scene exists in the Turner Bequest, and from it we cannot gauge what time of day or in what type of weather the artist witnessed the demolition. Yet obviously he took his dramatic cue from the fact that the building was demolished during the autumn, and further complemented the melancholy mood of the scene by portraying it in evening light (we are looking at the house from the south-west, with the light coming from the west) and with the dead tree in the foreground. All of these factors support a central meaning in the work: we are looking at the dying house of the dead poet in the dying part of the day and the dying part of the year, with a dead tree that alludes to Pope's own dead willow in the foreground.

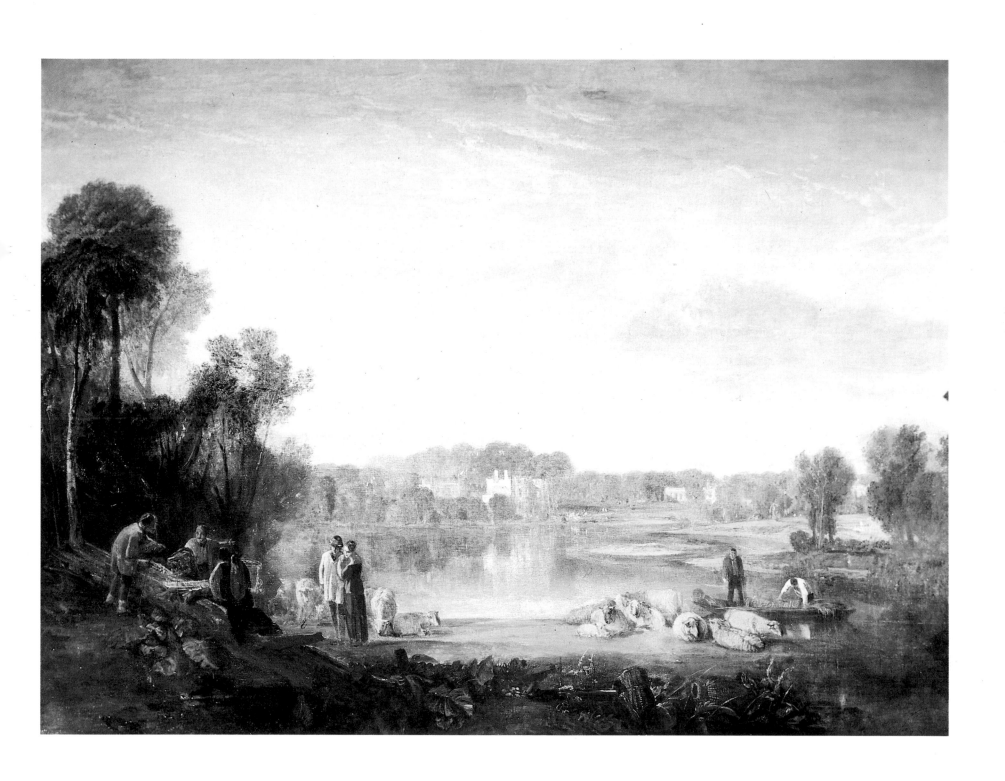

Snow Storm: Hannibal and his Army crossing the Alps, *1812*

146 × 237.5 cm. Clore Gallery for the Turner Collection, London

When this work was exhibited at the Royal Academy in 1812 its title was accompanied in the exhibition catalogue by the following verses:

> Craft, treachery, and fraud — Salassian force,
> Hung on the fainting rear! then Plunder seiz'd
> The victor and the captive, Saguntum's spoil,
> Alike, became their prey; still the chief advanc'd,
> Look'd on the sun with hope; — low, broad and wan;
> While the fierce archer of the downward year
> Stains Italy's blanch'd barrier with storms.
> In vain each pass, ensanguin'd deep with dead,
> Or rocky fragments, wide destruction roll'd.
> Still on Campania's fertile plains — he thought,
> But the loud breeze sob'd, 'Capua's joys beware!'

These verses were the first to have appeared in the Academy catalogue openly from Turner's pen, being drawn from his 'Fallacies of Hope' which never existed as an entire poem. The first line introduces the keynote of the picture — 'Craft, treachery and fraud' — and then indirectly tells us that Turner subscribed to the belief that Hannibal had crossed the alps by the Little Saint-Bernard Pass, for the territory of the Salassi was the upper Val d'Aosta, which the painter had visited in 1802. These Salassians are attacking both the Carthaginians and their captives from Saguntum, the Greco-Iberian city whose capture by Hannibal in 219 BC had brought about the second Punic war with Rome. However, Hannibal does not care what is happening to his rearguard but presses on, hoping to beat the coming winter and reach the south where he might defeat the Romans, although the wind warns him to beware of 'Capua's joys'. These will ultimately prove to be his downfall, for the fifteen years he would later spend luxuriating in Capua would sap his capacity to beat Rome and give the Romans the necessary breathing space in which to regain their strength and defeat him. Ultimately the painting is therefore a comment upon the irony of Hannibal's wasted efforts in crossing the alps and the futility of territorial aggrandizement. In the context of the war with Napoleon that was still continuing when this picture was painted, Turner's moral must have been directed at contemporary French expansionism.

On the right an avalanche cascades snow down into the pass; in the foreground the Salassi pick off stragglers and pitch boulders onto the Carthaginians. In the sky the sun is masked by dark clouds, an effect that is both naturalistic and metaphorical, for the 'clouds of war' (a metaphor that Turner was fond of realizing visually) are blotting out the sunlight of peace.

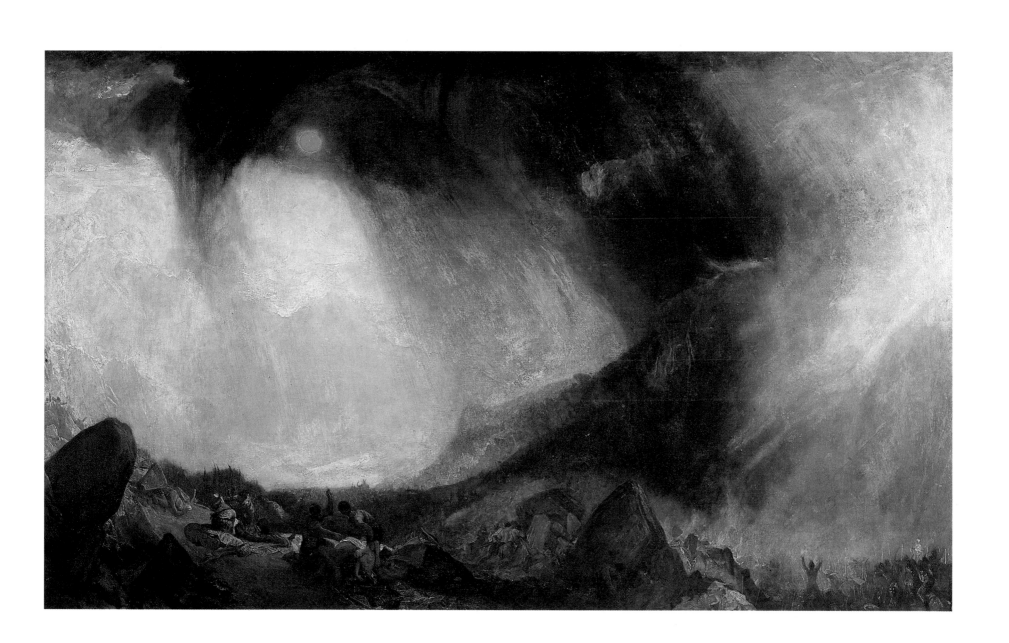

Dido building Carthage; or, the Rise of the Carthaginian Empire, 1815

155.5 × 232 cm. National Gallery, London

Turner considered this painting to be his masterpiece and for a time requested that he should be buried in it when he died (see Introduction). He exhibited the work at the Royal Academy in 1815 but never sold it and eventually bequeathed it to the National Gallery to hang alongside a view of a seaport by Claude. Although Turner had toyed with the idea of painting a Claudian seaport scene around 1806, not until 1815 was he ready to do so.

Queen Dido had fled from Tyre with the remains of her dead husband, Sychaeus, who had been murdered by her brother, and she founded a new city on the shores of North Africa. On the right is her husband's tomb; near it is a dead tree, while from it grows a sapling, indicating the growth of Carthage from the death of Sychaeus. Beyond them is the stately grove of trees that stood in the centre of Carthage, according to Virgil's *Aeneid* (from which Turner derived this subject). Beneath the tomb is a *cloaca* or drain conduit. In ancient times these had symbolized the future greatness and longevity of cities, as Turner knew from a book in his library. On the left are Queen Dido and a retinue of architects, builders and masons planning the new city which arises beyond them. In front of the queen, and wearing a dark cloak and helmet, is the only man standing in her presence, and he is almost certainly Aeneas, for at the point in Virgil's poem that inspired this painting the Trojan prince tours the newly-building Carthage but has yet to meet its queen. The fact that two masts are diagonally aligned with these two figures supports such an interpretation, for the masts dominate the harbour, just as Dido and Aeneas dominate everyone in it in terms of rank. In front of this group are some boys playing with toy boats, and they are watched by two nubile girls. These boys and girls may respectively personify power and generation, for the boys now playing with toy boats will soon sail the vessels that will exercise Carthaginian power in the Mediterranean, and the girls will provide them with the children who will later maintain that power.

In keeping with the fact that the city is rising the sun is also rising; such dramatic matching was known as 'Decorum' in the literature of art known to Turner and he observed it very often, as we have already witnessed in *Pope's Villa at Twickenham*. The composition is underpinned by a linear structure of taut, crossing diagonals, horizontals and verticals not unlike that of the basic layout of the Union Jack. These lines impart a great underlying strength that is not inappropriate to the subject. On the left all is teeming with life and energy; on the right all is still and deserted, an antithesis that adds to the dramatic range of the work.

66

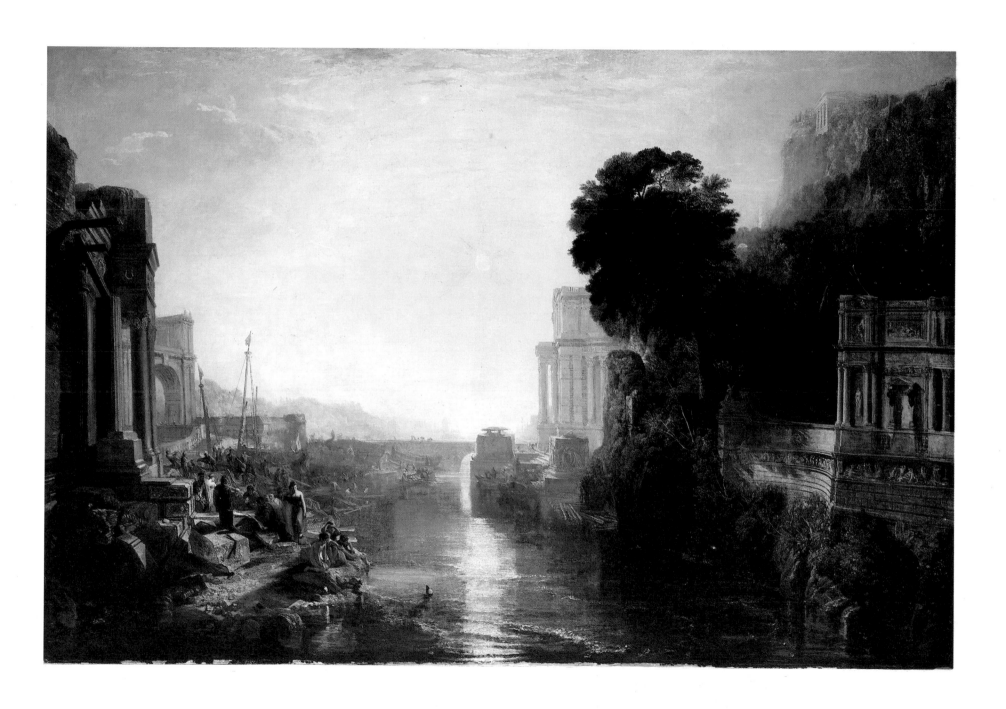

The Decline of the Carthaginian Empire, 1817

170 × 238.5 cm. Clore Gallery for the Turner Collection, London

This painting was exhibited at the Royal Academy in 1817 but it forms a pendant to the *Dido building Carthage* shown there two years earlier. Its full title is *The Decline of the Carthaginian Empire — Rome being determined on the Overthrow of her Hated Rival, demanded from her such Terms as might either force her into War, or ruin her by Compliance: the Enervated Carthaginians, in their Anxiety for Peace, consented to give up even their Arms and their Children.* This wording was further lengthened in the R.A. catalogue by further lines from Turner's 'Fallacies of Hope':

******At Hope's delusive smile,
The chieftain's safety and the mother's pride,
Were to th'insidious conqu'ror's grasp resign'd;
While o'er the western wave th'ensanguined sun,
In gathering haze a stormy signal spread,
And set portentous.

Here Turner depicted the moment between the second and third Punic wars when the Carthaginians, enfeebled by fifty years of peace, no longer had the will or the arms to stand up to the Romans and instead handed over 300 of their children as hostages; grieving mothers dot the scene, while luxury goods (including a garlanded painter's mahlstick) litter the foreground and further the associations of Carthaginian material-ism, the cause of their enervation.

As in *Dido building Carthage*, the underlying compositional structure matches the central dramatic sensibility of the work, for instead of the straight lines of the earlier picture we see a great number of circles, semicircles and ellipses that project a feeling of slackness. This structural flaccidity is furthered by the fact that the buildings throughout the work are not aligned on any rectilinear ground-plan but stand at all different angles to one another and therefore look disorientated.

In the distance the sun sets on Carthaginian power. Originally (according to Ruskin) the sky was much redder than it is today, thus introducing apt associations of blood.

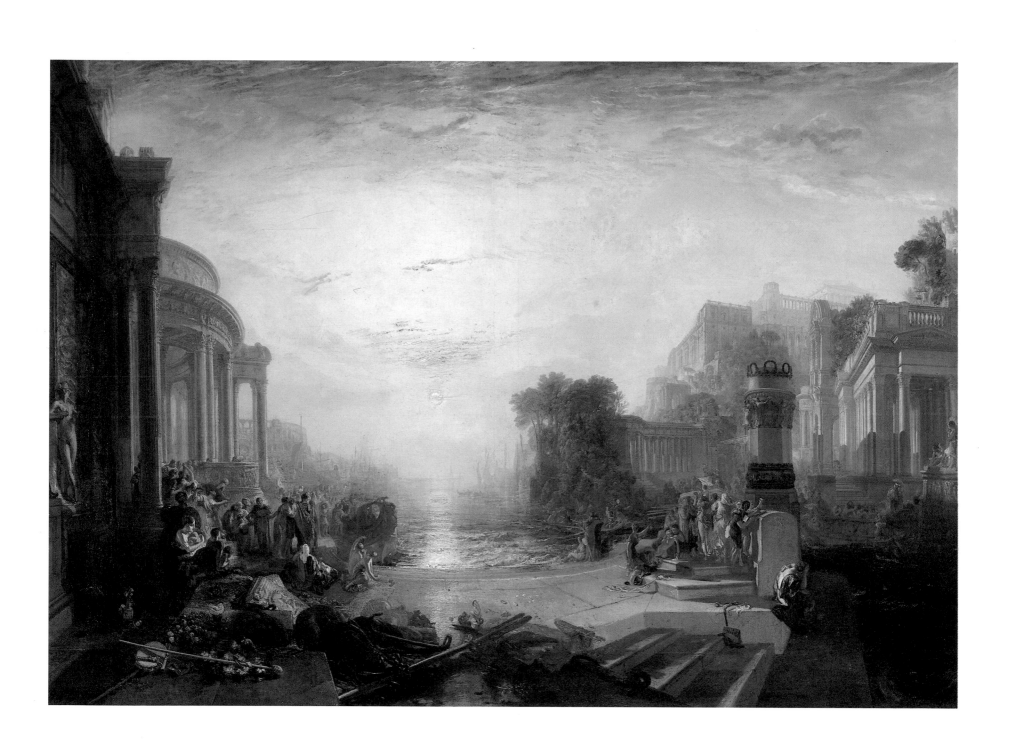

Crook of Lune, looking towards Hornby Castle, c. 1817

28 × 41.7 cm. Courtauld Institute of Art, University of London

Turner made this watercolour for line engraving in the 'History of Richmondshire', an ambitious part-work written by the Rev. Thomas Dunham Whitaker, a Lancashire cleric, tree-planter and antiquarian. Although 120 watercolours were commissioned from the artist, only twenty-one were made before the scheme was cancelled for lack of public support.

About four miles upstream from Lancaster the river Lune winds back on itself, and here we view that 'crook' in evening light. To the north-east and in the far distance near the top-right is Ingleborough hill (2373 ft/723 m) while directly opposite our viewpoint is Hornby Castle, a building that Turner represented twice more in the 'Richmondshire' series. Our attention is not only drawn to the distant castle by the fact that it directly faces us (as Turner's title makes clear), but also by its vertical alignment with the group of cattle feeding below it on the opposite bank of the Lune, with the man on a horse riding along the Lancaster road below them, and with the V-shaped declivity in the foreground next to the quarryman with his pick. This declivity pulls us into the scene, and its opposing diagonals parallel the diagonal bank of the Lune on the left and the diagonal line of the convoluted branch to the right, a branch whose twisting reinforces our apprehension of the curvature of the river. In the foreground the overall horizontality of the scene is broken by saplings whose elegant forms fully project their inner life. Such idealism subtly augments the ideal beauty of the landscape, the feeling that we are looking at a perfect world.

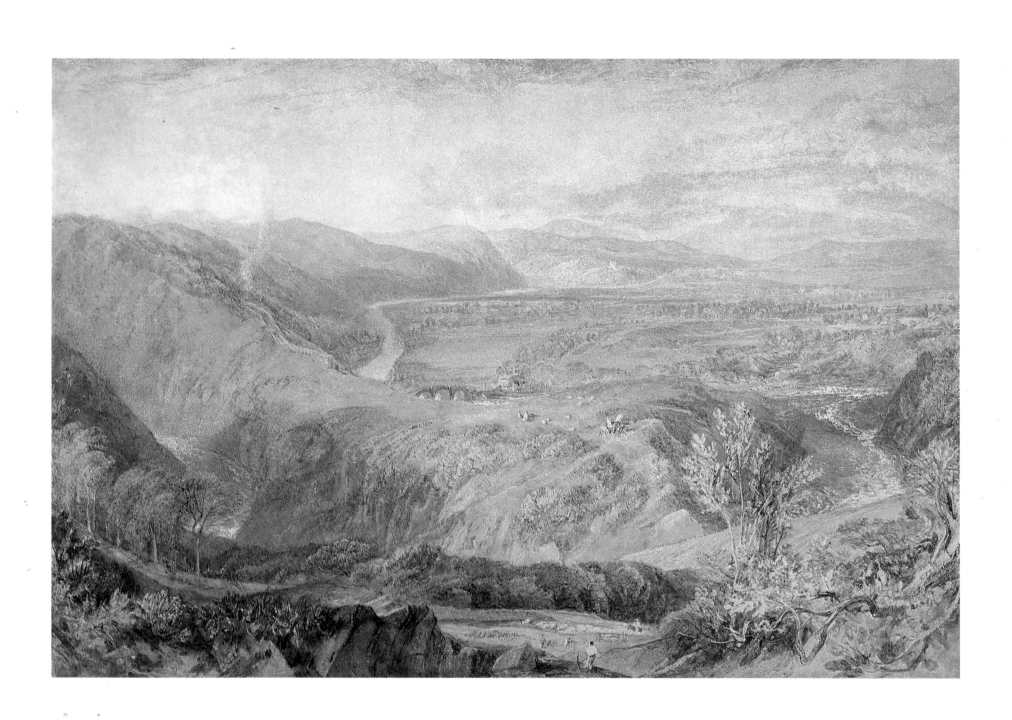

A First Rate taking in stores, 1818

28.6 × 39.7 cm. Cecil Higgins Art Gallery, Bedford

In Turner's day warships were rated according to the number of guns they carried; a 'First-Rate' was a ship of the line of battle that bore more than 110 guns.

Turner made this watercolour for his great patron and friend Walter Fawkes, and according to an account that was handed down in the Fawkes family, the Yorkshire-man said to the painter one morning at breakfast:

'I want you to make me a drawing of the ordinary dimensions that will give some idea of the size of a man of war'. The idea hit Turner's fancy, for with a chuckle he said to Walter Fawkes' eldest son [Francis Hawksworth Fawkes], then a boy of about 15, 'Come along Hawkey and we will see what we can do for Papa', and the boy sat by his side the whole morning and witnessed the evolution of 'The First Rate Taking in Stores'. His description of the way Turner went to work was very extraordinary; he began by pouring wet paint onto the paper till it was saturated, he tore, he scratched, he scrubbed at it in a kind of frenzy and the whole thing was chaos — but gradually and as if by magic the lovely ship, with all its exquisite minutiae, came into being and by luncheon time the drawing was taken down in triumph. I have heard my Uncle give these particulars dozens of times . . .

Turner made the man-of-war tower over us by merely showing us part of the battleship and by adopting a very low viewpoint. He also boosted the vessel in size internally, for judging by the seamen leaning out from the lower gun-deck, its gun-ports are about 10 ft high (in reality they would have been as small as possible in order to prevent enemy projectiles from entering the ship). However, the gun-ports diminish greatly in size as they ascend, and that enforced perspective subtly increases the overall sense of scale, which is equally enhanced by the contrasting smallness of the adjacent boats, one of which flies the Dutch flag.

In the distance two further men-of-war are softly outlined, one of them glistening in the moist air. Their drifting angle to one another vividly conveys the immense, lumbering bulk of such vast warships. On the sea can be witnessed Turner's extensive use of stopping-out varnish, a masking fluid that is painted on and worked over before being rubbed off afterwards to reveal the virgin paper underneath. Highlights were also sparingly added with gouache or scratched out with Turner's thumbnail, which he kept especially sharpened for the purpose.

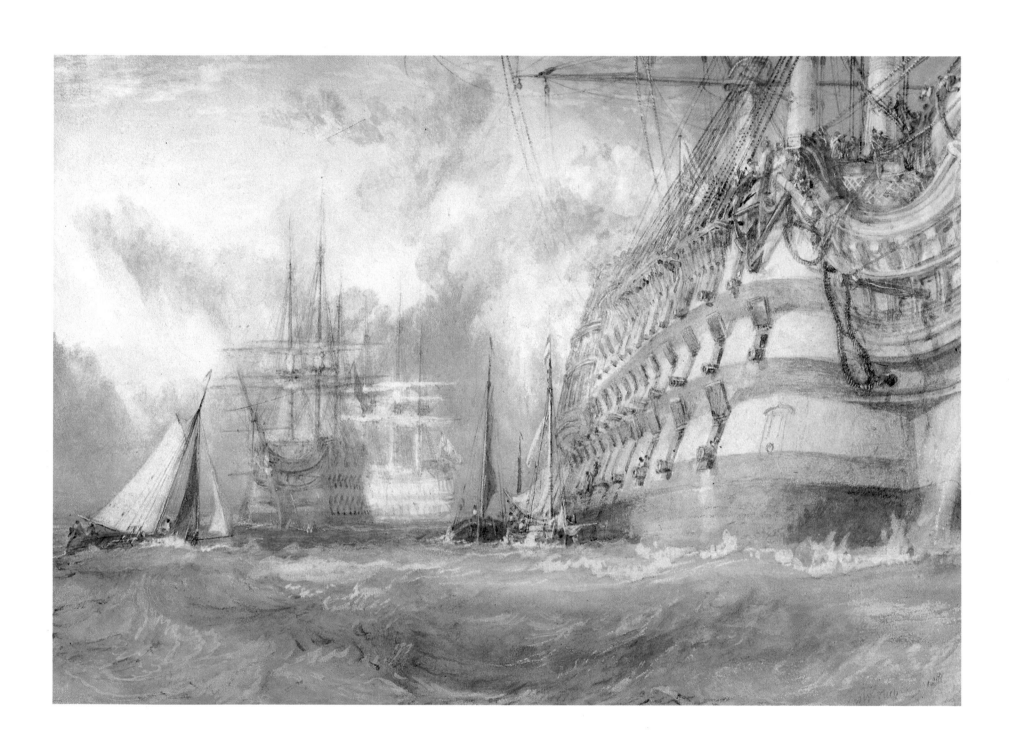

England: Richmond Hill on the Prince Regent's Birthday, 1819

180 × 334.5 cm. Clore Gallery for the Turner Collection, London

Turner had known the view from Richmond Hill since his youth, and made many watercolours of it both before and after creating this painting, which was exhibited at the Royal Academy in 1819. In the catalogue its title was accompanied by lines drawn from James Thomson's poem *The Seasons*, verses that were actually inscribed on a board affixed to a tree at the top of Richmond Hill in Turner's day.

It has recently been demonstrated that this painting portrays a large garden party that was given on Tuesday, 12 August 1817 in private grounds on Richmond Hill by the Dowager Countess of Cardigan to celebrate the Prince Regent's birthday. Turner could not have been present at the party as he had sailed for the Continent two days earlier, but the newspapers reported it in great detail, and the preparations had naturally involved a great many people for several weeks beforehand both in Richmond and in the adjacent Twickenham (where Sandycombe Lodge was located). Given that by 1817–19 Turner had reconstructed Greek, Carthaginian and Roman scenes, he would certainly have had no problem in reconstructing events on his own doorstep. And his own link with the landscape is signalled far above the discarded drum in the right-foreground, where the top of a tree just intersects with the horizon, for that meeting-point indicates the location of Sandycombe Lodge.

The Prince Regent attended the 1817 soirée, as did other members of the Royal Family and the Lord Mayor of London. Although none of those dignitaries is visible, the Lord Mayor's barge is discernible on the Thames, while in the centre some people seem to be gossiping about a woman who stands staring out at us. She may allude to the estranged wife of the Prince Regent, Princess Caroline, who was the subject of much gossip in the late 1810s. On the right are the 'petararoes' or small cannon which were fired in honour of the Prince when the Royal health was drunk, and also apparent are retainers in court dress, an army recruitment with a soldier beating a drum, and an officer in uniform on the right. A cello and a portfolio introduce associations of the arts. A great many women are viewed from behind, and their elongated necks are reminiscent of similar forms seen in the works of Watteau and Fuseli; the connection with Watteau is a particularly appropriate one, for the French painter had often projected an ideal existence that Turner surely emulated here. There is also an obvious connection with Claude in the layout of the work, although Turner has perhaps even gone beyond him in his projection of a perfect world. The trees look especially ideal, and they are surely the arboreal equivalent of the perfected human forms of, say, Praxiteles or Michelangelo.

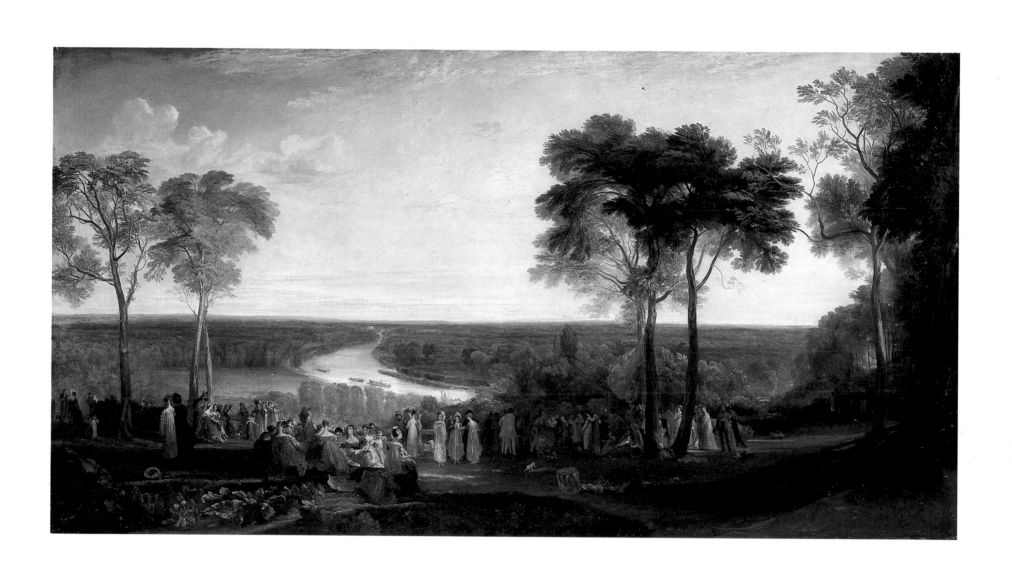

MARXBOURG and BRUGBERG on the RHINE, 1820

29.1 × 45.8 cm. British Museum, London

The title given above, with its upper and lower case spelling, is Turner's inscription on the drawing itself, which is also dated. His gallic 'Marxbourg' is Marksburg Castle, seen in the distance, while his 'Brugberg' is Braubach, the village located at its foot which is situated just below the junction of the Rhine and Lahn rivers, about seven miles south of Coblenz. Turner had visited the spot on his Rhineland tour of 1817, when he made a watercolour on grey paper (now in the Indianapolis Museum of Art) from which he later developed this drawing for a member of the Swinburne family.

The artist was at his most idealistic here. We view the scene in evening light, with a girl holding a bushel of wheat on her head and pointing to the nearby wheatfield, another girl with an empty pannier, and a young man who has been pushing a loaded barrow taking a break to quench his thirst. In the distance, and across a much wider expanse of fields than existed in reality, may be seen the Rhine. And the expansion of the banks of the river is not the only liberty that Turner took with reality here, for in actuality Marksburg Castle is surrounded by hills that are of a similar height or lower. Turner has expanded those hills into large mountains, and added further mountains beyond them so that they form part of an alpine chain. On the left a normally rolling hillside was transformed into a sheer rock face that disappears out of the top of the design, and rather like the battleship in *A First Rate taking in stores*, its implied extension beyond the image does much to add to its huge sense of scale. That towering quality is subtly augmented by the nearby ash trees whose tops are not visible either. Judging by the size of the foreground figures, the trunks of these trees below their first branches are each about 25 ft high, which would make their total height immense. But Turner was not concerned with literal appearances in this watercolour. Instead he gave full rein to his fancy, endowing all his trees with a sense of their inner life and locating them in a world that is infinitely larger and more beautiful than the mundane one we inhabit.

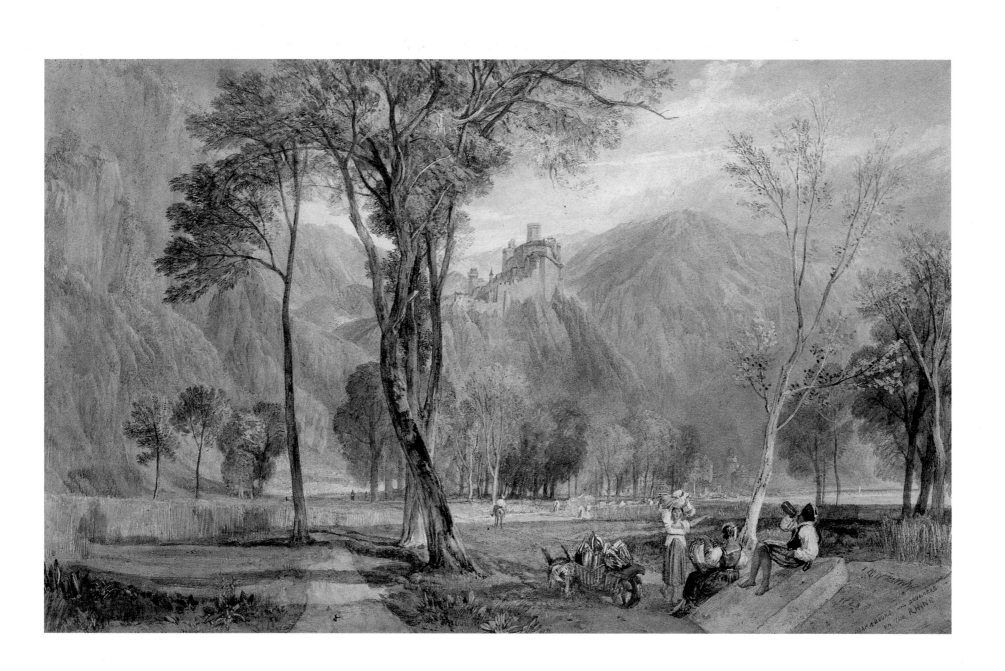

Dover Castle, 1822

43.2 × 62.9 cm. Museum of Fine Arts, Boston

In this magnificent watercolour Turner celebrated the coming of the age of Steam. At the mouth of Dover harbour various fishing vessels, including the lugger on the left, are finding it difficult to enter port because of the prevailing westerly wind. To avoid being blown out to sea they are therefore reducing sail, although because there is insufficient room to tack, the vessels on the right will either have to wait for the turn of the tide or row into harbour. But ignoring all these problems is a paddle steamer which is cutting easily through the prevailing wind. On the north pier a group of figures waves its excitement upon seeing this new form of transport, while some boys and a dog run away, their movement extending the impetus of the steamer.

This steamship had originally been built as a sailing vessel, for she has a beak-head prow and a sailing hull. Just beyond her is a wrecked brig, a juxtaposition that comments on the replacement of wind-propulsion by steam, the steamer looking as if she has just pushed aside the brig. Cross-channel steamers were still very topical when this drawing was made, for although the *Majestic* had been the first such vessel to cross the channel in 1816, only in 1821 did the *Rob Roy* pioneer regular crossings. The foremast and funnel of the steamer are aligned with the towers of the Roman Pharos (lighthouse) and the church of St Mary in Castro above them on the East Cliffs, and that pairing is repeated by the masts of the wrecked brig and by the twin sails of the lugger in front of the steamer. Before the steamship a tiller and a partially-submerged rudder resemble an axe in overall shape, perhaps to augment our sense of the steamer cutting through the wind.

In this work Turner again contrasted British inventiveness and seamanship with the poor seamanship of foreigners. The steamer sports the blue ensign while the lugger on the left flies a foreign flag. The lugger is in trouble, for because of her crew's failure to properly stow sails used previously while fishing, the deck is awash with canvas. As a result, her helmsman is trapped between the canvas and an arched gallows used to support the foremast when lowered. He therefore has no room to pull the tiller hard over to starboard, as he needs to do urgently in order to turn the vessel around to the left and thus avoid colliding with the boat passing in front of him. Although his fellow crew members are shouting at him or are dismayed at what is happening, there is little he can do, and the collision seems inevitable.

The movement of the sea and the reflections upon it are painted with Turner's usual grasp of the underlying truths of form and appearances, as are the castle and cliffs in the damp, late-afternoon sunlight.

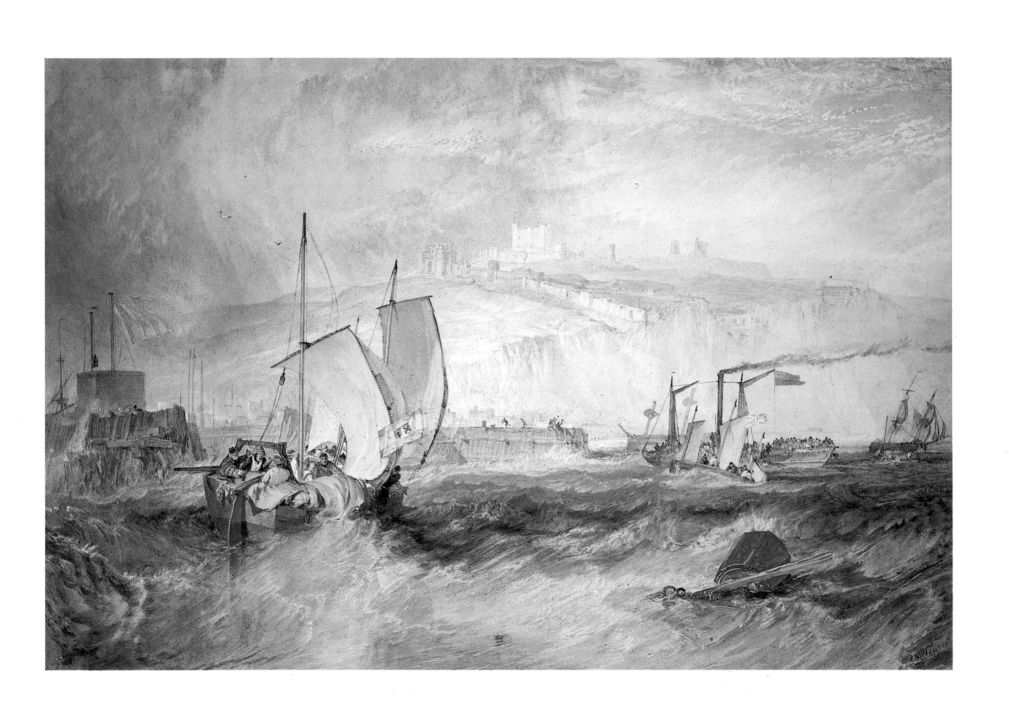

The Storm (Shipwreck), 1823

43.4 × 63.2 cm. British Museum, London

Like *Dover Castle* above, this watercolour was made for engraving in a series entitled 'Marine Views'. Turner created some eight drawings for this scheme between 1822 and 1824 and also allowed an earlier design to be included, but only two of the engravings were completed during his lifetime. When the drawing was exhibited by the engraver W.B. Cooke in his London gallery in 1823 it was titled *The Storm*; in Cooke's account book and in a contemporary review it was known as *Shipwreck*, so both titles are given here. The fact that it was given generalized titles like these indicates that Turner was portraying an imaginary storm and shipwreck.

This is undoubtedly the most ferocious seascape that Turner ever painted in watercolour and it is difficult to believe that anyone could survive in such a maelstrom. The plunging surges of the sea, the berserk fury of the sky, the brilliant colouring and dynamic linearity, all communicate a world gone mad with energy, in which a doll-like mankind struggles pathetically to survive.

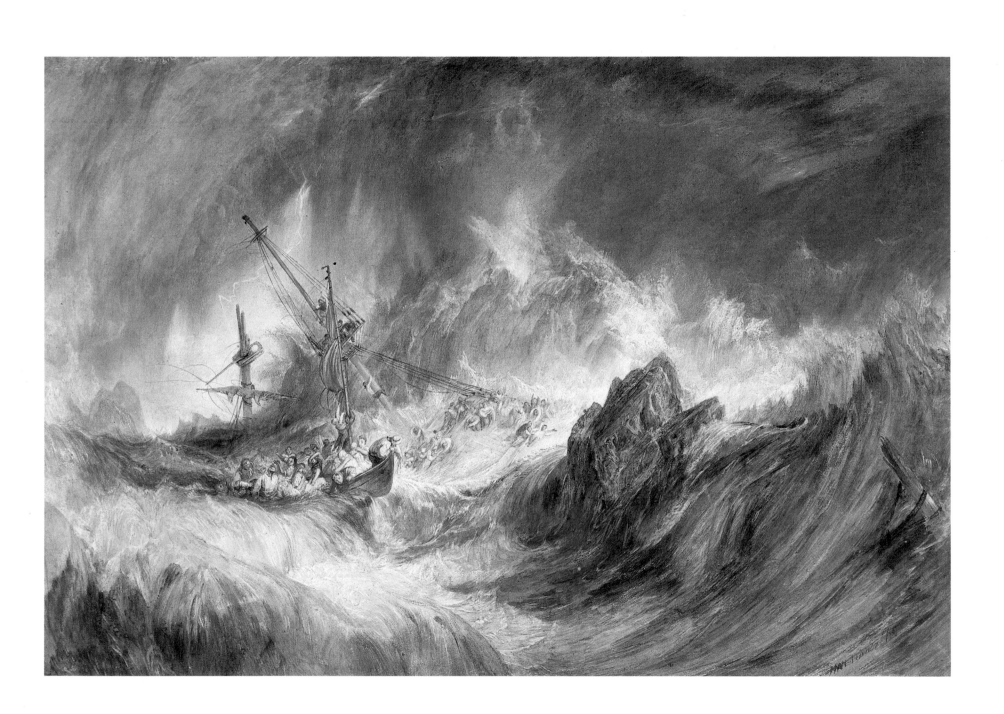

Rye, Sussex, c. 1823

14.5 × 22.7 cm. National Museum of Wales, Cardiff

This watercolour was made for engraving in Turner's first great set of topographical prints, the series of forty designs created between 1811 and 1825 entitled 'Picturesque Views on the Southern Coast of England'. The engravings were published by two brothers, William Bernard and George Cooke, and originally the 'Southern Coast' scheme was to have formed only the first section of a four-part project that would have encompassed the entire coastline of Great Britain. However, a dispute between Turner and the engravers in 1826 meant that the more grandiose venture unfortunately never came to fruition. The painter went on to make a number of watercolours for a continuation of the scheme up the east coast of England, and even had some of the designs engraved himself, although they were never published.

During the Napoleonic wars it was feared that Romney Marsh and the lowlands to the west might be the site of an enemy invasion, owing to their proximity to France. As a result, between 1804 and 1809 an extensive defensive system comprising forts known as Martello towers, and a canal and road respectively known as the Royal Military Canal and Road, were built across the whole area. Between Rye and Winchelsea the river Brede served in place of the defensive canal, and it was reinforced by the Royal Military Road which ran parallel with it for most of its length; beyond Winchelsea the canal continued the defence line westwards. Turner appears to have visited the area around 1805–7 and seen the fortifications under construction.

Here we look eastwards from Winchelsea towards Rye along the Royal Military Road, with the Strand Bridge at Winchelsea to the left; the river Brede runs across the scene in the mid-distance. A spring tide has just swept along the river and overwhelmed a temporary wooden dam which had been built to facilitate construction work on a further, westward leg of the Royal Military Canal at the bottom-right. On the Royal Military Road a man on a cart urges on his horses while men run off in the opposite direction; immediately in front of us more workmen cling to the timber shuttering of the demolished dam in order to avoid being carried away by the sudden tidal surge.

In the distance, to the right of Rye, are Camber Castle and the sea. With his usual penchant for exaggeration Turner made Rye much bigger than it is in reality. Throughout the sky and the tidal flow along the river, there is an appreciable sense of energy expressed through a multitude of flowing, swirling lines. Yet these lines not only impart meteorological and hydrodynamic energies; their constant twists and turns also help project the panic felt by all the men as they attempt to save their lives.

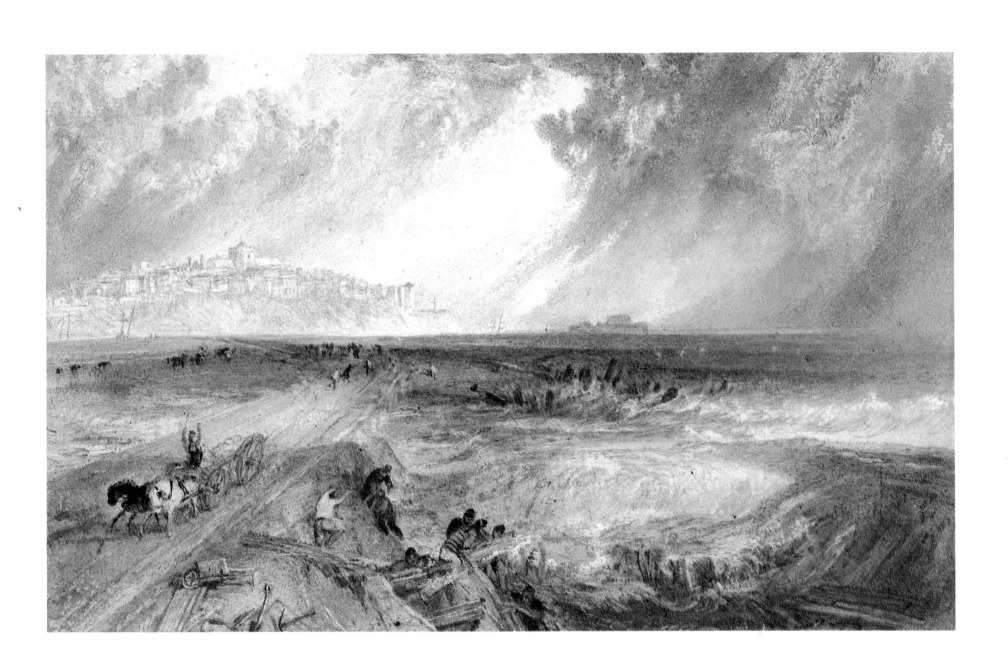

The Battle of Trafalgar, 1822–1824

259 × 365.8 cm. National Maritime Museum, Greenwich

This is the largest picture that Turner ever painted and it resulted from the only Royal commission he ever received. The work was ordered by King George IV to hang in St James's Palace alongside de Loutherbourg's *The Glorious First of June*, and also to complement two further battle scenes of Vittoria and Waterloo by Turner's friend George Jones. The commission itself was probably obtained through the offices of the President of the Royal Academy, Sir Thomas Lawrence.

In order to garner factual material on the ships that had participated in the battle, Turner borrowed sketches from the marine painter J.C. Schetky, although he already possessed studies of Nelson's flagship, the *Victory*, which he had obtained after Nelson's body was returned home in 1805. When the work went on view in St James's Palace Turner was severely criticized for having made a number of errors in the rigging of the various ships and other nautical details, and he spent some eleven days altering the work to meet those criticisms, including lowering the *Victory* in the water, for Schetky had sketched the ship when she was unladen in Portsmouth harbour. Yet even after meeting these criticisms the painting continued to mystify Turner's very literal-minded naval contemporaries (including the Duke of Clarence, later King William IV), principally because the artist had followed the demands of the theory of poetic painting to evade the limitations of time. As a result, we see events that took place hours apart, such as the signalling of the last word from Nelson's famous telegraphic message 'England expects every man to do his duty' which had gone up around midday, alongside the collapse of the top-mizzenmast of the *Victory* which occurred at 1 pm, the *Achille* on fire off the *Victory* which took place late in the afternoon, and the *Redoubtable* sinking in front of the *Victory* which did not happen until the following night (and even then it sank elsewhere). Naturally, these manipulations of the constraints of time were not welcomed by an audience who wanted 'the facts, the facts and nothing but the facts'; well might Turner have responded by citing Michelangelo's riposte to a critic of one of his effigies that it looked nothing like the person it was meant to portray: 'Well, in a thousand years time nobody will know the difference.'

The foreground filled with carnage might not have helped public acceptance of the work either, for such anti-war sentiments would not have been popular with most naval viewers. The low viewpoint makes the men-of-war tower up over us, and their vast billowing sails serve to express the immense forces unleashed by war.

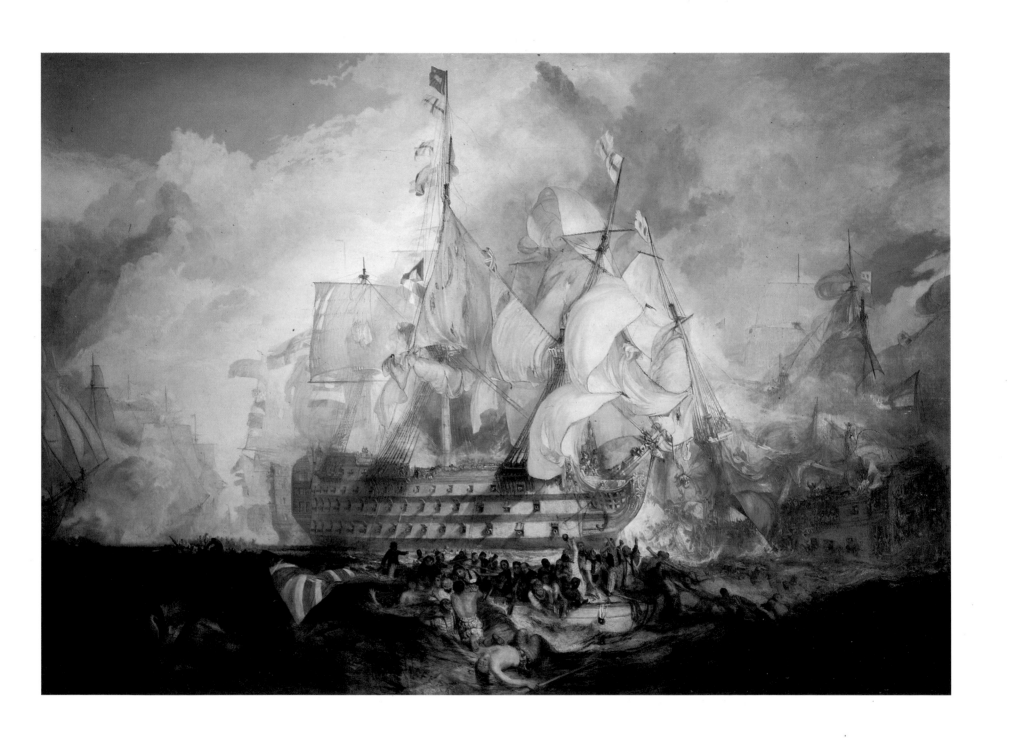

Portsmouth, 1825

16 × 24 cm. Clore Gallery for the Turner Collection, London

Turner made this watercolour for engraving in 'The Ports of England' series, a scheme that never reached completion owing to a quarrel between Turner and the engraver, Thomas Lupton. The painter created at least sixteen watercolours for the series, although only seven of the designs were published as engravings during his lifetime. In 1856, five years after his death, the seven engravings and six more prints after drawings made for the project were republished or newly published by Lupton under the title 'The Harbours of England', with an accompanying text by Ruskin.

In the early-morning light a man-of-war prepares to make for sea and it towers over the harbour and town as the very embodiment of naval grandeur. Turner made the vessel much bigger than it would have been in reality, and its vastness is boosted by the small vessels placed before it, for they augment its scale by contrast. The captain's pennant on the battleship, its billowing sails and the sails of the cutter on the right all indicate that a strong north-westerly breeze is blowing, which explains the choppy motion of the water in the distance, while the rotundity of a nearby buoy reinforces the sweeping motion of the wave on the left.

On the tower to the right, above the cutter, is the Admiralty Semaphore. This supported a signal which could communicate with the Admiralty in London in under three minutes by means of a series of intermediate semaphores. The device had proven very useful during the Napoleonic wars when Turner had visited Portsmouth. In front of the semaphore is a sailor whose straw-hat points directly at it. The connection of his boater and the semaphore is subtly established by the parallel diagonal lines of the cutter's main-yard and the shadow in the sky beyond it, parallels which pull the eye up to the right. The curve of the sailor's waving arm is also repeated and reinforced by the curve of the cutter's mainsail, thus connecting them. By signalling to the battleship the sailor personifies naval communications, just as his waving gesture communicates a sense of heroic urgency.

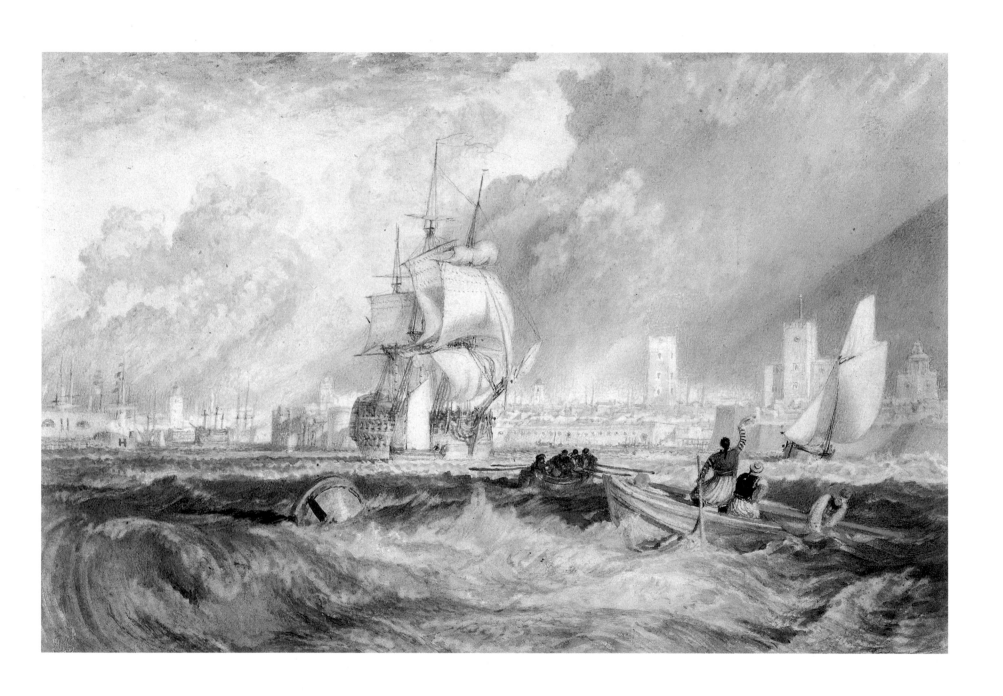

Prudhoe Castle, Northumberland, c. 1825

29.2 × 40.8 cm. British Museum, London

This watercolour was made for engraving in the most ambitious topographical scheme that Turner was ever involved in, the 'Picturesque Views in England and Wales' series. Although 120 designs were commissioned for the venture, in the end only about 100 were produced before the project was terminated in 1838 owing to a lack of public support. The 'England and Wales' series watercolours perhaps constitute the finest set of watercolours that Turner ever made for engraving.

Prudhoe Castle in Northumberland stands on a small hill by the river Tyne about ten miles inland from Newcastle, a distance indicated by the 'X' placed on a milestone at the bottom-left hand corner of the design. Turner based this drawing upon sketches made at Prudhoe in 1817 soon after he had returned from his tour of the Rhineland, and the influence of Rhenish scenery might explain why he made the castle tower over the Tyne as it does here, instead of appearing more modestly as it does in reality. Naturally the influence of Claude Lorrain is apparent, but the trees on the right are equally a necessary tonal foil to the brilliance of the distant moors beyond. Three overlapping triangles subtly structure the composition, one of them forming the road on the right and the others dividing the river into two channels, the right-hand one denoting the usual course of the Tyne and the left-hand one the course it took when flooded.

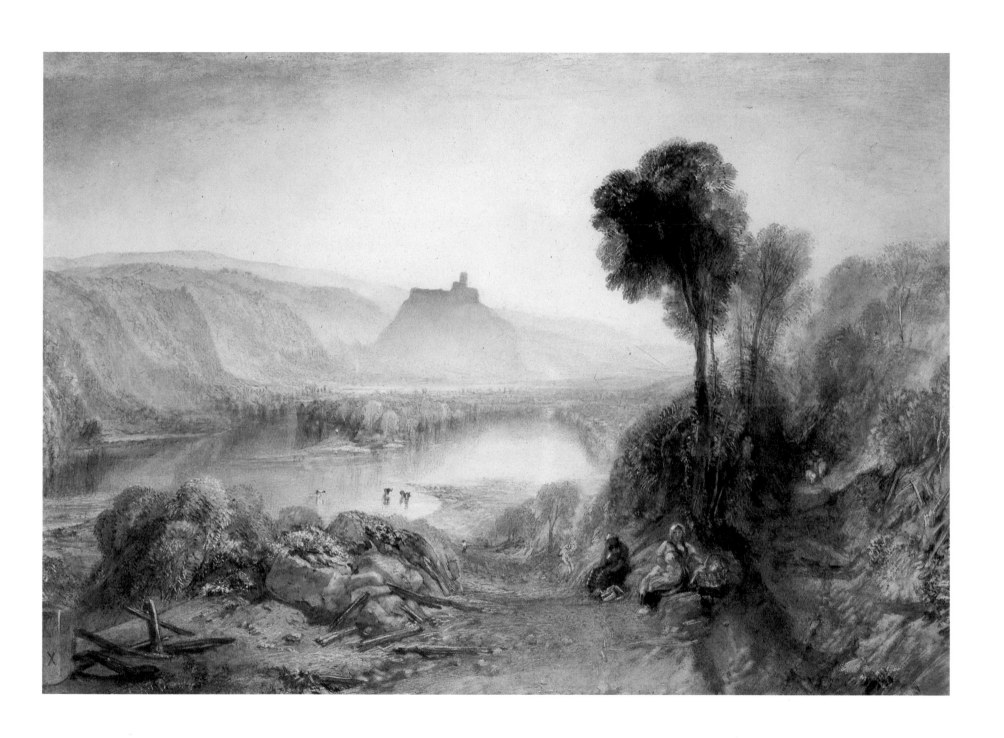

Forum Romanum, for Mr Soane's Museum, 1826

145.5 × 237.5 cm. Clore Gallery for the Turner Collection, London

Turner visited Italy in 1819–20 and this painting, which he exhibited at the Royal Academy in 1826, is one of the loveliest products of that trip. As its title indicates, it was commissioned by Sir John Soane, an architect and fellow Royal Academician. However, in the event it proved to be too large for Soane's house and although Soane honoured his commitment by paying for the picture with a banker's draft for 500 guineas, the artist did not cash the draft but retained the work instead. Soane later bought another painting.

We survey the scene in afternoon light. On the left, in front of the Palatine Hill, is the Arch of Titus dating from AD 81, with the three columns of the Temple of Castor and Pollux visible through it, and Turner also exercised considerable poetic licence to bring a number of buildings into view from behind the arch. On the right is the Basilica of Constantine, and further off is the line of buildings that are ranged along the Via Sacra and which pass beyond the Capitoline Hill. The vaulting across the top of the picture that does so much to unify it structurally is completely invented.

Under the Arch of Titus a girl kneels in prayer before a monk; in the distance monks bearing holy banners follow the Host being carried beneath a canopy to the Church of San Lorenzo in Miranda. In front of the distant monks and next to other, kneeling figures is a two-wheeled cart which introduces associations of a tumbril, perhaps as an allusion to the sufferings of the early Christians or more generally to introduce apt associations of death within such a dead part of Rome.

In this painting Turner not only responded to the beauty of the Roman forum but equally he projected his sadness at its prevailing desolation. And the solitary girl in the foreground who rests her head in her hand seems to personify that sadness, for her pose is the one that Turner habitually used to denote sorrow, while with her other hand the girl idly plucks the odd note on a discarded lute. Just like the Roman forum her music is cast down, disconnected and forlorn.

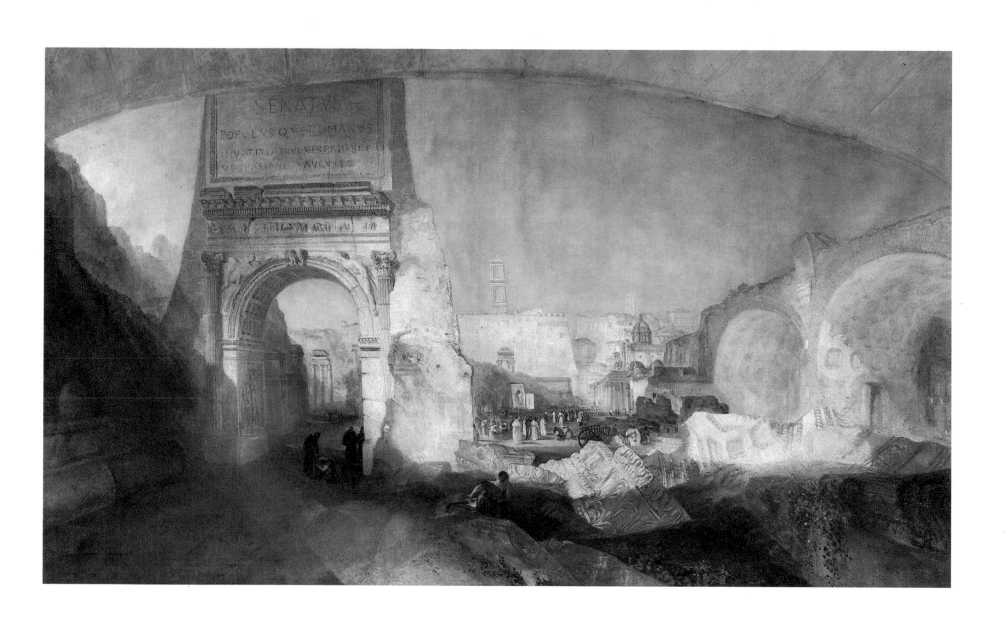

Mortlake Terrace, the Seat of William Moffatt, Esq. Summer's Evening, 1827

92 × 122 cm. National Gallery of Art, Washington DC

This is one of a pair of pictures commissioned by William Moffatt and it was displayed at the Royal Academy in 1827, the companion having been exhibited there the previous year. In the pendant (which is now in the Frick Collection, New York), Turner portrayed the view in morning light looking towards William Moffatt's house, 'The Limes', a building that took its name from the avenues of lime trees standing in front of it which were all cut down in 1896. Here we look from the house at the other end of the day.

The brilliant evening light is reflected off the parapet and that glare is intensified by the contrasting dark shape of an adjacent dog. For many years a story circulated that this dog had been pasted on and overpainted by Edwin Landseer who felt that the picture needed such a strong focal point, but the tale is almost certainly untrue. What surely happened was that Turner himself originally cut the dog out of paper (and the parasol next to it), stuck them onto the canvas and then painted over them, a procedure he is known to have used on other occasions. Unfortunately the paper dog then became detached on one of the Varnishing Days at the Academy in 1827, falling to the floor. Landseer must have seen this, pasted the dog or a replacement back on again temporarily, and then went and found Turner who was lunching elsewhere in the building to tell him of what had happened. Turner thereafter returned from lunch, '. . . went up to the picture unconcernedly, never said a word, adjusted the little dog perfectly, and then varnished the paper and began painting it. And there it is to the present day'. Only this would explain Turner's unconcern at somebody tampering with one of his pictures, and in any case it seems impossible that the twenty-four-year-old Landseer would have had the temerity to add to a painting by one of the most senior and respected Academicians, any more than that Turner would have permitted such a liberty.

On the river is a Royal barge; the King and other members of the Royal family regularly used the Thames between London and Windsor as it was the most comfortable way to get from the one place to the other. The London plane trees in this picture are among Turner's most ideal arboreal forms, their inner life and energy running along every sinuous line of trunk and branch, and through each gentle shadowing of foliage.

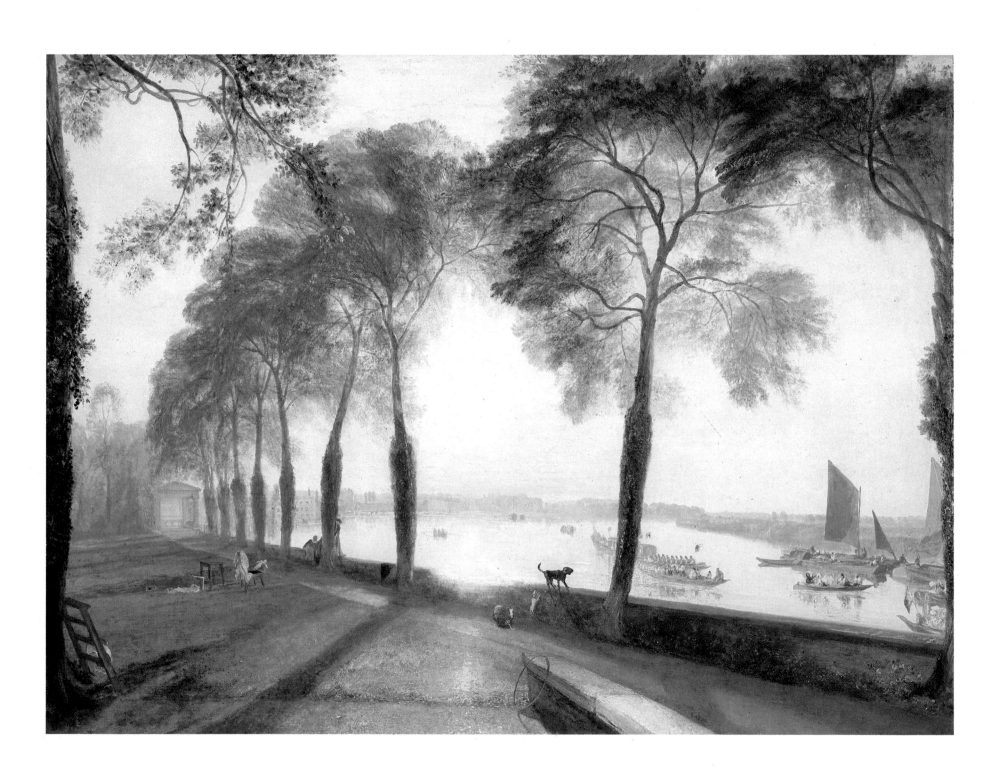

Petworth Park: Tillington Church in the Distance, c. 1828

64.5 × 145.5 cm. Clore Gallery for the Turner Collection, London

George Wyndham, the third Earl of Egremont and owner of Petworth House in Sussex, was a rather eccentric, kind-hearted and paternalistic Tory of the old school, whose moral views were sufficiently elastic to allow him to have numerous mistresses and innumerable illegitimate children. He also owned nine pet dogs. Turner painted several views of Petworth Park for the nobleman, as well as depictions of the newly-built Chichester Canal and the Chain Pier at Brighton (in both of which the earl had invested), while for his own pleasure the painter made a great many watercolours of the hustle and bustle of daily life in Petworth House, superb studies filled with light and movement. The present oil sketch was made as a study for an oil painting that was commissioned by Lord Egremont, and at one time it hung at Petworth, presumably so that the patron could gauge the effect of the final picture. The staffage is quite different in the later work.

Here Turner portrayed Lord Egremont himself. On the extreme left is the wall of Petworth House, with a chair standing in front of it. This juxtaposition of a country seat with a 'country seat' may pictorialize a play on words (Turner loved visual puns), while the man leading the dogs was described by Turner's contemporary, Thomas Creevey (who saw the work hanging at Petworth in 1828), as 'Lord Egremont taking a walk with nine dogs, that are his constant companions'. The fact that Egremont makes his way towards the sunset could be symbolic, for from the 1820s Turner repeatedly made a connection between the coming of night and the coming of death, and the aged Egremont was certainly amid the last blaze of life and approaching his twilight years when this lovely picture was painted.

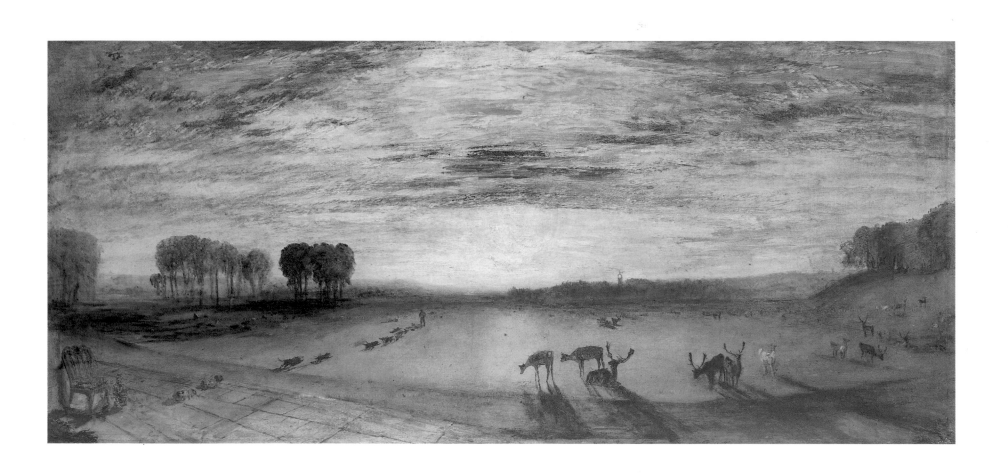

Ulysses deriding Polyphemus — Homer's Odyssey, 1829

132.5 × 203 cm. National Gallery, London

In Book IX of Homer's *Odyssey*, Odysseus (of which Ulysses is the Latinized form) is trapped with twelve of his crew in the cave of the one-eyed giant, the Cyclops, who eats two of the men every dawn and dusk. After getting the giant drunk, Ulysses and his remaining companions blind the Cyclops at dawn by poking out his eye with a sharpened, heated stake, whereupon they escape from the cave by clinging to the undersides of a flock of sheep and rams belonging to the giant.

At the top-left the blinded Cyclops clutches his head in one hand and waves his other fist in anger; far below him Ulysses stands by the mizzenmast of his ship and 'derides' him. On the mainmast of the vessel is a flag bearing the name of Odysseus in Greek, and another representing the Trojan horse. On the left of the ship is a fiery cavern; this may appropriately have been intended to link the Cyclops with primeval subterranean forces. On the horizon the sun-god Apollo is pulled aloft in his chariot, and still discernible are the heads of his horses, a device that Turner probably borrowed from Poussin's painting *Cephalus and Aurora* and from contemporary engravings of the east pediment of the Parthenon. At the prow of Ulysses' vessel are phosphorescent nereids holding aloft stars, Phosphorus being the son of Aurora (who symbolizes Dawn) and thus the personification of the morning star. This area of luminescence demonstrates Turner's concern with all types of visual phenomena, just as his continuing interest in reflected light can be witnessed in the gorgeous colours of the shadowed side of Ulysses' ship.

It is usually assumed that Turner represented the actual escape of Ulysses in this painting, but that is incorrect, for the Greek hero has rejoined his fleet (a linkup that occurs later in the poem) and he is following his other vessels, as is made clear by the wakes of those ships at the bottom of the picture. Moreover, when Ulysses does escape, the Cyclops hurls huge boulders down into the sea after him, and again, those rocks are not visible, although the great rock-arches in the distance may allude to them. Instead we see Ulysses at dawn on the day *after* his escape, the time given by Homer for him to sail away from the land of the Cyclops.

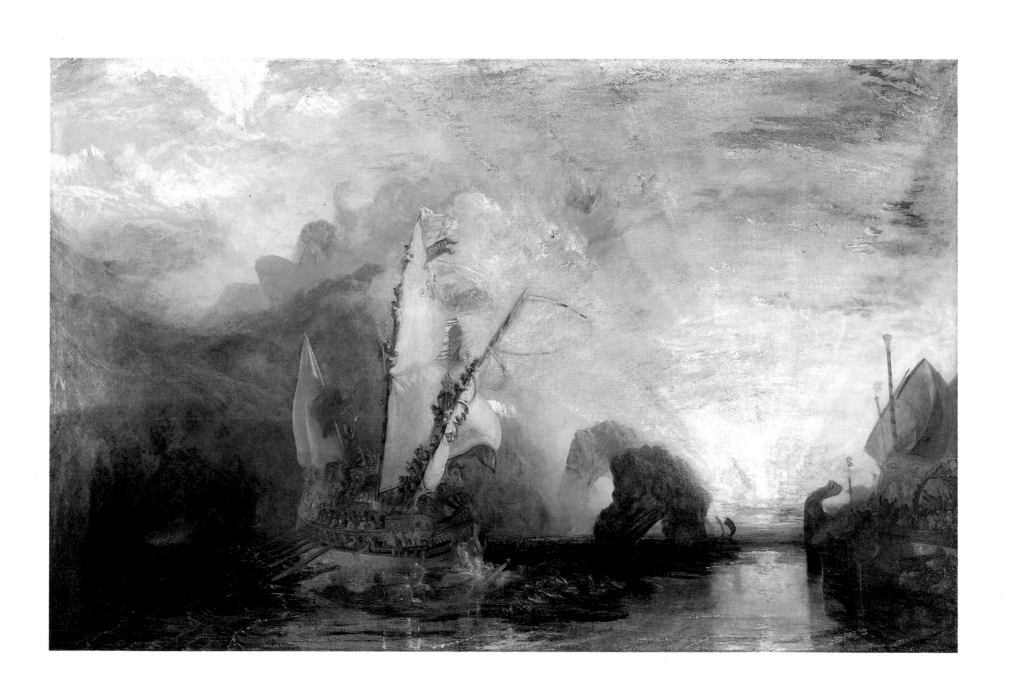

Scio (Fontana de Melek, Mehmet Pasha), c. 1832

Private Collection

This vignette watercolour represents a drinking fountain that still stands in Plateia Vounaki, the main square of the town of Chios on the Greek island of that name. It was built in 1768 by Pasha Mehmet Melek, a Vizier or governor of the island and later a high-ranking minister in the Turkish Imperial Curia. In the distance on the right stands the church of the Monastery of the Predicator, with a mosque beyond. The drawing was one of nineteen designs that were made for engraving in an edition of the complete works of Lord Byron published between 1832 and 1834, and Turner, who never visited Greece, developed it from a sketch by William Page (1794–1872), a minor professional topographer. The vignette was used to illustrate the volume containing Cantos 1–3 of Don Juan, although the poem only briefly alludes to Chios under its archaic name 'Scio' (hence the title of the work).

The drawing demonstrates how Turner could invest even the most seemingly inconsequential works with complex meanings. In 1822, after a small insurrection on Chios during the Greek War of Liberation, the Turks who controlled the island had shocked Europe by massacring some 25,000 of its inhabitants, an event perhaps best remembered today by Delacroix's famous painting of the atrocity. After the killings had ended the Turks sold 47,000 of the remaining Chiots into slavery (severely depressing the market price of slaves in the process) and leaving only about 1000 people living on the island.

By 1832, around which date Turner made this watercolour, Greece had been an independent state for some two years, and therefore he made the scene a peaceful one. On the right a Turk and a Greek converse peaceably together, while in the centre-foreground lies a discarded yoke, an obvious allusion to the fact that by now the yoke of Turkish rule had been thrown off. On the left a seated woman with her head in her hand strikes the traditional pose denoting grief that Turner customarily used, and she obviously and most appropriately alludes to the recent tragic history of the island, particularly as she is placed immediately beyond another yoked figure passing out of sight behind two women chatting contentedly.

Turner was wholly aware of Byron's political idealism, and he had openly identified with the cause of Greek independence long before it had been attained. This outwardly unpromising subject must therefore have afforded the painter a welcome opportunity to comment upon the final achievement of Greek freedom and peace.

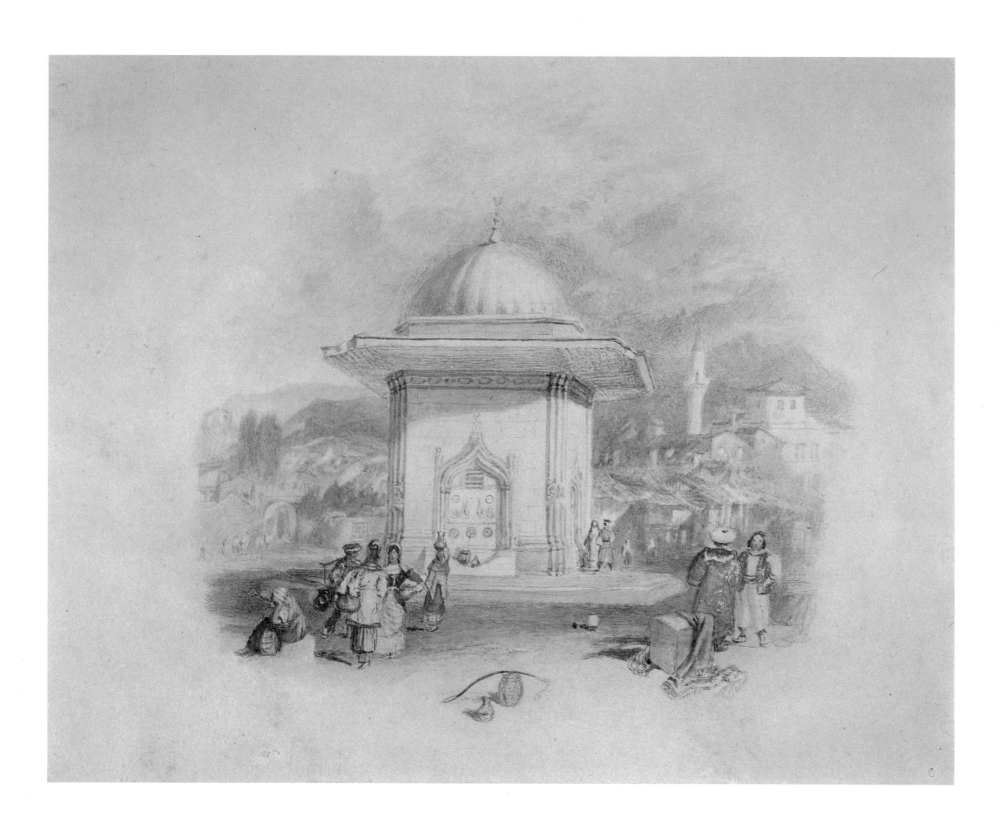

Loch Coriskin, c. 1832

8.9 × 14.3 cm. National Gallery of Scotland, Edinburgh

Turner was at his busiest producing watercolours for engraving during the 1830s, and several of them were created to adorn an edition of the complete *Poetical Works* of Sir Walter Scott published in twelve volumes in 1834. For each volume Turner produced a vignette for the title page and a rectangular frontispiece design to appear opposite; this drawing was made for the latter purpose and appeared as the frontispiece to Volume X, in which was published 'The Lord of the Isles'. In order to obtain fresh material for the Scott illustrations, Turner had visited Scotland in 1831 and stayed for part of the time with the ailing author and poet before going on to the Highlands and the western isles.

In 'The Lord of the Isles' Scott described Loch Coruisk or 'Coriskin' as a forbidding place:

. . . rarely human eye has known
A scene so stern as that dread lake,
With its dark ledge of barren stone.
Seems that primeval earthquake's sway
Hath rent a strange and shatter'd way
Through the rude bosom of the hill.
And that each naked precipice,
Sable ravine, and dark abyss,
Tells of the outrage still.

Turner was not someone to pass by a place like that, and on his 1831 tour he made for Oban, whence he caught a steamer to Elgol on the Isle of Skye and then took a boat across to the mouth of Loch Coruisk. In his watercolour the painter compressed the scene, so that we look up Loch Coruisk towards Sgurr Thuilm (2884 ft/879 m) in the distance on the right, and up the adjacent coastline and valley towards Sgurr Alasdair (3309 ft/1008 m) on the left, with Sgurr na Banachdich (3167 ft/965 m) in the centre. Everywhere through these vast rock formations Turner has made immediately evident their geological idealities of form, the great stratifications and fissurings that tell 'of the outrage still'.

In the foreground two tiny figures set off the enormity of the scene by contrast. One of them is clearly Turner himself, sketching the view, while the other would be the boatman who had rowed him across Loch Scavaig from Elgol. Turner later told the publisher of Scott's *Poetical Works*, Robert Cadell, that he had almost been seriously injured (or worse) at Loch Coruisk, for he missed his footing while negotiating its slopes and, 'but for *one* or *two* tufts of grass', would have 'broken his neck'. Had he done so we would have been deprived of *The Fighting 'Temeraire'* and a host of other masterpieces.

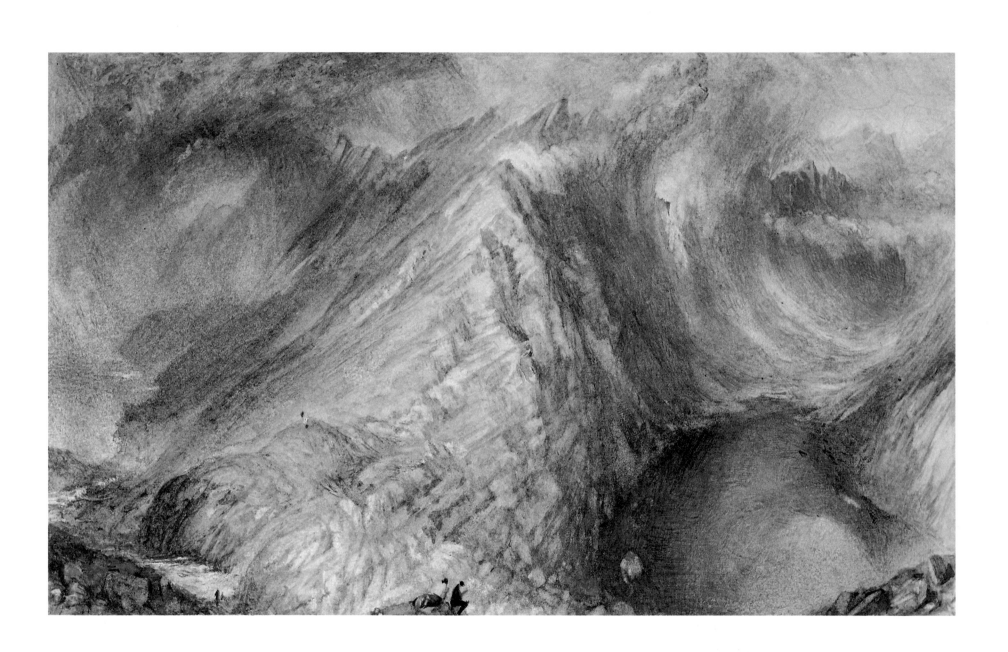

Mouth of the Seine, Quille-Bouef, 1833

91.5 × 123.2 cm. Fundaçao Calouste Gulbenkian, Lisbon

In the distance is the lighthouse at the mouth of the Seine, and the adjacent church and churchyard at Quillebeuf. Turner was very attracted to the place, for he visited it on four separate tours of France, made two colour studies of it in watercolour and also worked up a watercolour of it on blue paper for engraving in a part-work published in 1834, *Turner's Annual Tour — The Seine*.

When this painting was exhibited at the Royal Academy in 1833 the following note was appended to its title in the catalogue:

> This estuary is so dangerous from its quicksands, that any vessel taking the ground is liable to be stranded and overwhelmed by the rising tide, which rushes in one wave. This wave is known locally as the '*Mascaret*' or '*Barre*'.

To Turner, lighthouses were mostly symbols of the failure of human hopes, for nearly all his lighthouses have failed in their purpose, being surrounded by wreckage and/or drowning figures. If combined with a church, as here, one might equally be tempted to interpret the lighthouse as denoting the futility of religious hope as well. But in this superb painting the lighthouse has *not* failed in its purpose, and instead both lighthouse and church shine brilliantly in the bleak, early evening sunlight. In conjunction with the dangers that we are reminded of verbally by Turner in his accompanying caption, it appears that for once the artist was regarding a lighthouse and church as beacons of hope, which of course they were in reality.

The composition is unified by a superb arabesque line which runs down the flock of gulls on the left, around to the column of water created by the tidal bore clashing with an oceanic wave in the centre, and up along the edge of the cloud beyond. The sharp contrast of evening sunlight with dark storm-clouds gives the picture an immense sense of both spatial and tonal depth, and the dampness in the atmosphere is tangible. When the work was displayed in 1833 the critic of the *Morning Chronicle* wrote that it made you '. . . long for a parasol, and put you in fear of the yellow fever, and into a suspicion of the jaundice', but the orange colouring is just what one would see towards sunset with a reddish sun presumably nearing the horizon off to the right.

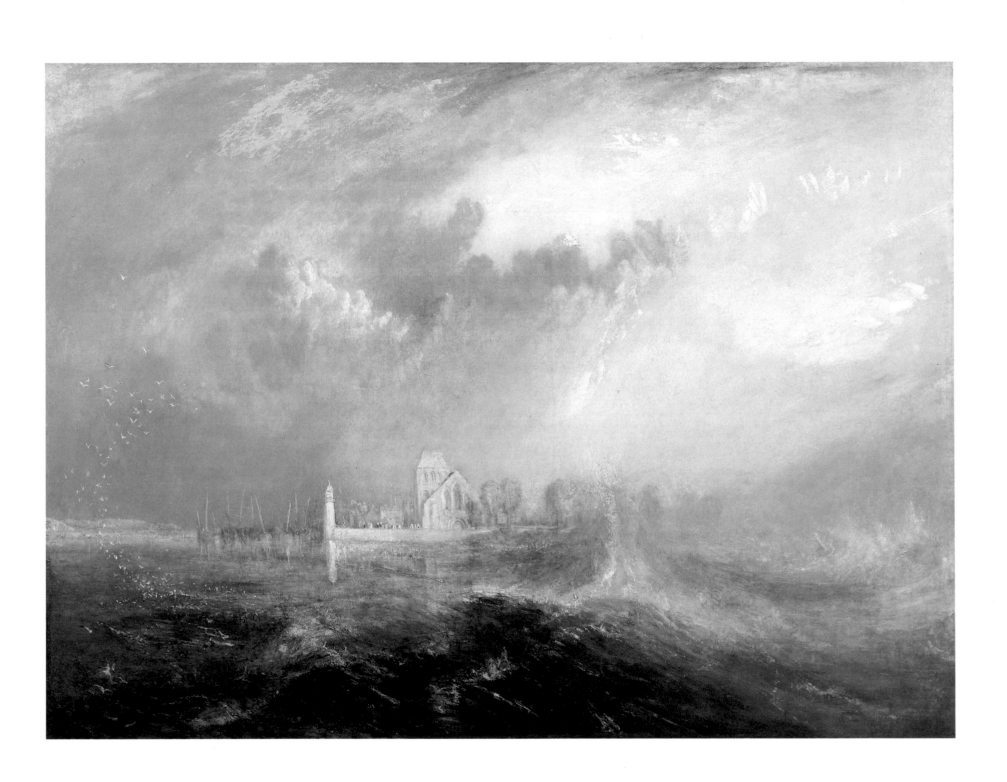

The Golden Bough, 1834

104 × 163.5 cm. Clore Gallery for the Turner Collection, London

This view of Lake Avernus in Italy was exhibited at the Royal Academy in 1834. Turner had already represented the same scene twice before he ever went to Italy, once around 1798 when he worked up a painting of it from sketches made on the spot by Sir Richard Colt Hoare (who had commissioned the watercolours of Salisbury discussed above), and again around 1815. In both works Turner complemented the landscape with figures taken from Virgil's *Aeneid*, namely Aeneas and Deiphobe, the Cumaean Sibyl. In both of those paintings the Sibyl is giving Aeneas the golden bough that he needed in order to return from visiting his dead father in the land of the dead, the Underworld. However, in this work the Cumaean Sibyl is seen alone, holding the golden bough on the left.

On the extreme left is a statue of the Virgin Mary in a blue aureole niche; this refers to the fact that since the time of the early Christians it has been believed that the Cumaean Sibyl had prophesied the coming of Christ. Yet although the Sibyl is holding aloft a means of evading death, the absence of Aeneas (who cannot be visiting his father, for he would need the golden bough in order to return) makes it clear that Turner was not depicting the story of Aeneas and the Sibyl here, but rather that he was using the story of the golden bough to make a wider point about the indifference of mankind to its own ultimate fate. Instead of presenting Aeneas with the golden bough, the Cumaean Sibyl is proffering it to some dancers and nudes who are surrounded by luxury goods. Clearly, the indifference of these people to an object that would allow them to escape from the inevitability of their own deaths typifies a wider human indifference to mortality, while their attraction to hedonism and material things suggests why they are so unconcerned.

Moreover, Turner may even have wanted to create a parallel between the golden bough and his own *Golden Bough* here, for of course he believed that a work of art confers immortality, just as the magic branches being proffered by the Cumaean Sibyl were believed to have done so in classical antiquity. In *The Golden Bough* Turner was not only perhaps warning mankind of its mortality; it could well be that he was also celebrating the power of art and the art-object to triumph over death.

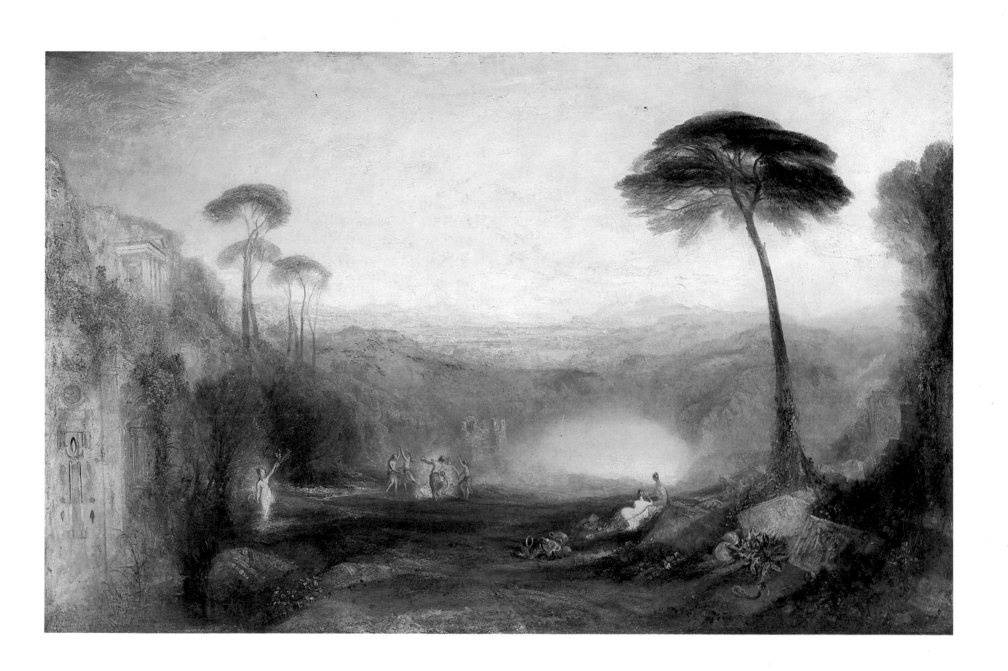

Venice, from the Porch of Madonna della Salute, 1835

91.4 × 122 cm. Metropolitan Museum of Art, New York

Turner first visited Venice in 1819, and made a number of impressive watercolours of the city both then and in the years which immediately followed, as well as planning a large oil painting of the Grand Canal from the Rialto, a work he only ever roughly sketched out on canvas. But in the 1833 Royal Academy show he exhibited a painting of Venice which was worked up from sketches made in 1819, and that reliance upon old sketches and memories seems to have spurred the artist to revisit the city later that year. Thereafter the majority of Turner's views of Italian scenery are of Venice. The present painting was exhibited at the Royal Academy in 1835. In it we look eastwards in late-afternoon light along the Grand Canal, and despite the title *towards* the portico of the Church of Santa Maria della Salute on the right.

The Grand Canal has been doubled in width, and that is not the only change that Turner made to reality here. Apart from his normal enhancements of space and scale, in this painting and in others like it Turner effected two major alterations to what he had witnessed in Venice. When the artist visited the city in the 1830s it was still a rather impoverished place, for it had never fully recovered from the French occupation in 1797. That occupation had not only put an end to the existence of Venice as an independent republic, but it also seriously damaged its economy for many years by curbing the tourism that had been its major industry in latter days. Although visitors returned to Venice after 1815 they did not do so in the same numbers as before 1797, and even in the 1840s writers on the city were commenting on its 'ghostly and funeral silence'.

However, that is not the Venice that Turner projected in his late works. Instead, from 1833 onwards he loaded Venetian boats to the gunwales with expensive-looking fabrics and other luxury goods because by such means he could introduce associations with the kind of wealth that had originally made Venice great, and the indulgence in luxury that had led to its downfall.

Turner's other major change affected the visual appearance of Venice. By intensifying the tonal dazzle of the buildings along the canals and by lengthening their reflections on water the painter greatly enhanced the floating quality of Venetian architecture. That disembodiment seems entirely apt, given that usually we gain our dominant perceptions of Venice by floating through it. Turner was therefore once again addressing the ideality of a place.

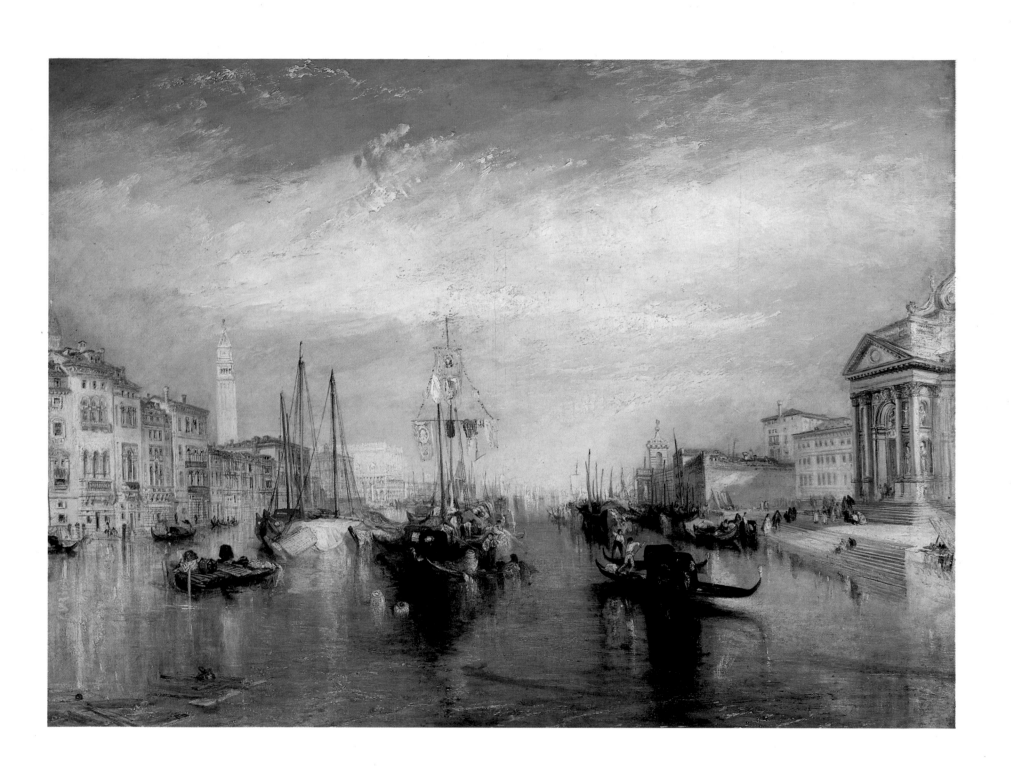

The Burning of the Houses of Lords and Commons, 16th October 1834, Exh. 1835

92 × 123 cm. Philadelphia Museum of Art

We know from the diary of an art student that Turner witnessed the burning of the Houses of Parliament on the night of 16 October 1834 from a boat on the Thames, along with another Academician and some further students from the Royal Academy Schools. This is one of four works that he made of the fire, and another oil painting of the subject was exhibited at the Royal Academy in 1835. That picture is now in the Cleveland Museum of Art and it also depicts the fire from the south bank of the river Thames but from a more distant vantage point, by Waterloo Bridge rather than Westminster Bridge, as here. A tiny vignette watercolour shows the scene from underneath Westminster Bridge and it was made for engraving in an annual book, *The Keepsake*, while a watercolour showing the fire in close-up from across New Palace Yard was probably made for the 'England and Wales' series but never engraved there. As related in the Introduction, the present work was largely painted on the walls of the British Institution, a feat that was highly admired by those fortunate enough to witness it.

In the distance the fire blazes up brilliantly, showering sparks across a starry sky. Turner took his usual liberties with topography here by extending Westminster Bridge so that it becomes about a mile long, and he also deformed it into a hump-backed bridge in the process. Swarming across the bridge and both banks of the river are the vast crowds who in reality turned out to watch the blaze. Not all of them would have been dismayed by the fire, however, for in the autumn of 1834 Parliament was discussing the Poor Law Act which would bring into being the workhouse system, and there were many people in Britain who felt that the fire was a divine verdict on such socially divisive legislation. Indeed, the word 'NO' is clearly visible on a placard in the centre-foreground, and it may refer to popular opposition to the Poor Law Act.

At the bottom-left a number of people kneel in supplication to a figure wearing medieval religious garb. He may perhaps allude to men such as John Wyclif and Sir Thomas More who had once struggled to extend British liberties, a concept that had some relevance to Parliament (and Turner had either depicted those men or alluded to them on earlier occasions). Maybe the supplicants are expressing their hope that the spirit of British liberty will not be lost by the destruction of the palace that housed the legislature.

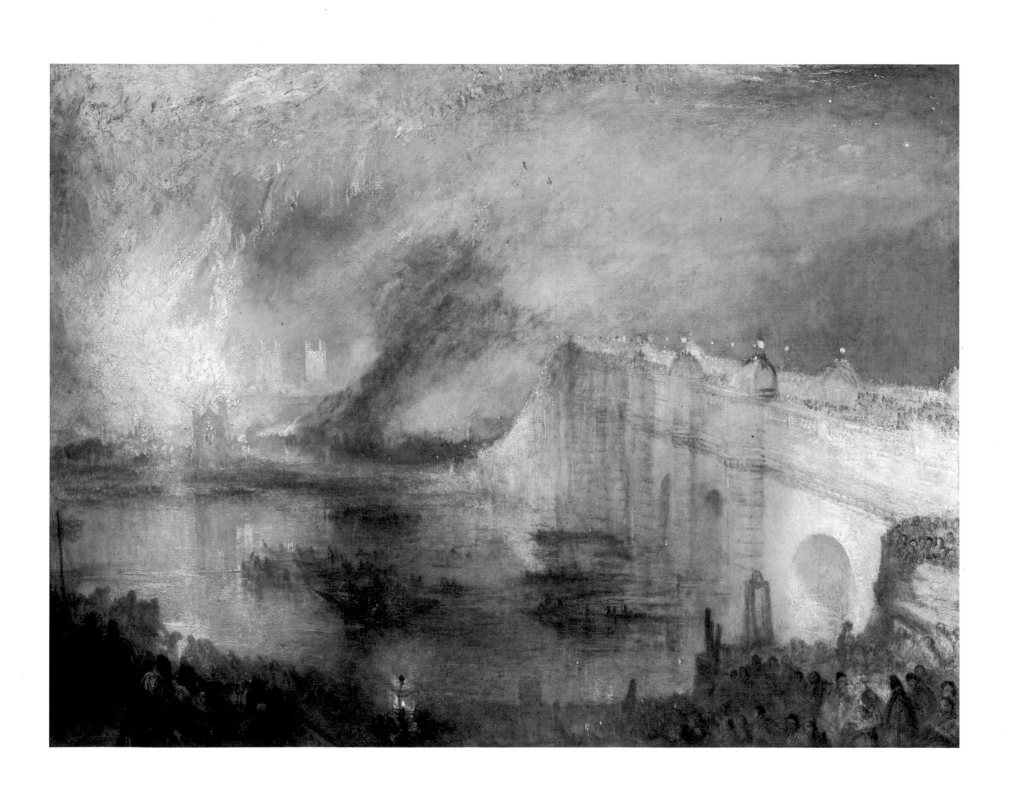

Flint Castle, North Wales, 1835

26.5 × 39.1 cm. Private Collection

This is one of the final watercolours that Turner made for the 'England and Wales' series, and it is also one of the finest drawings he ever made. Although Ruskin thought it to be a sunset and Turner took his usual liberties with topography here, nonetheless it is probably a dawn scene. Sunsets came to have tragic implications for Turner from the 1820s onwards through their association with the coming of night, and thus with death, as well as through their possible blood-red colour (two examples of such linkages will be given below), whereas here the mood seems to be a very happy one. In the distance the sun cuts into the horizon but there is no sign of the Wirral peninsula, the far bank of the estuary of the river Dee which we would see from this spot in reality, and this omission has also led to uncertainty as to whether we are looking inland (and thus at dawn) or towards the open sea (at sunset).

Turner had first visited Flint Castle in 1794, on his second tour of Wales, and in 1795 and 1797 two of his watercolour views of it were engraved. In 1807 a portrayal of the castle with vessels unloading in the foreground was published in the first part of the 'Liber Studiorum', and in the 1820s he made a lovely watercolour of the castle as a wedding present for a friend. And in this drawing he brought all of his earlier responses to Flint Castle and its environs to a triumphant conclusion.

As the mists rise from the beach at low tide and the sky fills with a multitude of colours a shrimper makes his way towards the sun with his creel raised in front of him. To the right another shrimper apparently offers a shrimp to a child. The strong shocks of vermilion and emerald green in the foreground greatly boost the colouristic brilliance of the work, while throwing into relief the subtle colouring of the distance. Similarly, the dark tones of the nearby shrimper's clothing and of the anchor and broken basket beyond him also augment the tonal delicacy of the distance, and thus our sense of immense space in the work. Just so that we do not forget that Flint Castle is a ruin, Turner has placed the timbers of a wrecked boat in front of it.

The artist's technical confidence can be seen at full stretch in this watercolour. Probably by using a damp sponge, he simply wiped out the sun and its reflection from an initial basic colour wash, and elsewhere the work was similarly underpainted with broad washes of soft yellows, reds, blues and greens which were all allowed to run into each other. The details were added later, and the highlights scratched from the paper.

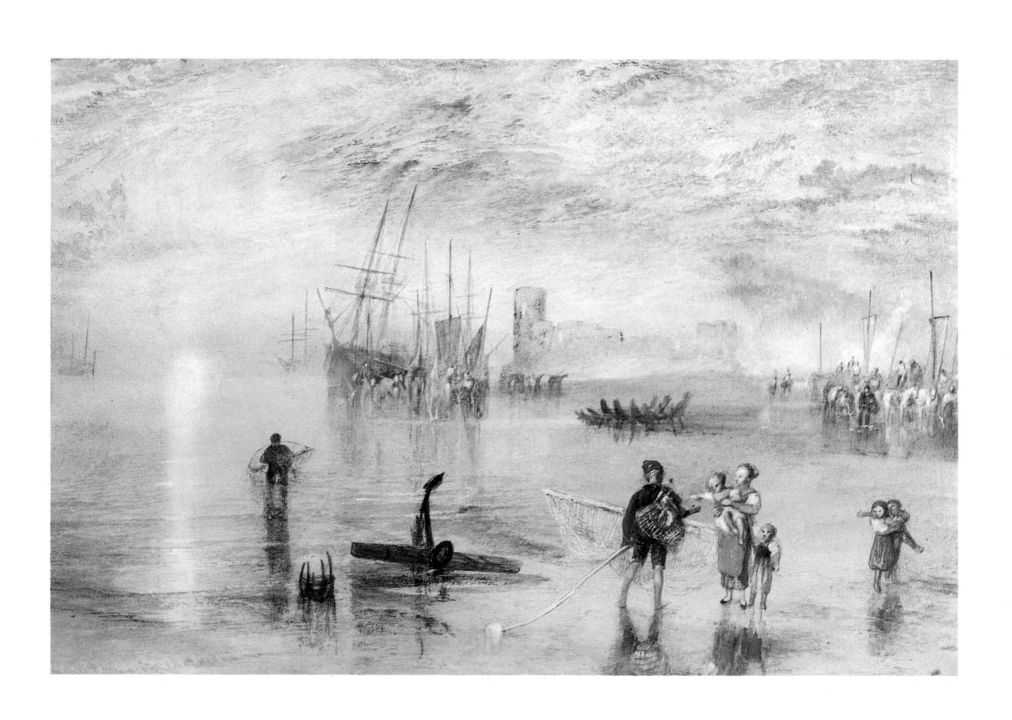

Snow storm, Avalanche and Inundation — a Scene in the Upper Part of Val d'Aouste, Piedmont, 1837

91.5 × 122.5 cm. Art Institute of Chicago

In the summer of 1836 Turner toured the Val d'Aosta in northern Italy with his friend and patron, H.A.J. Munro, who later owned this painting. The work was exhibited at the Royal Academy in 1837. Although Turner clearly had poor weather on the 1836 trip (judging by the many watercolours and sketches he made then), it must be doubted that he saw a snowstorm or avalanche that summer, let alone anything quite as cataclysmic as this.

The landscape represented here is probably not a particular one but rather a generalized scene drawing upon the artist's overall impressions of the upper Val d'Aosta looking northwards towards the Mont Blanc massif; the theory of poetic painting to which Turner subscribed certainly permitted artists to generalize from actualities, and of course he had often done so since his youth. The painting is also very much an exercise in the Sublime mode, with mankind dwarfed by the darkness, immensity and violence of external nature, although as was customary by now, Turner married the Sublime to the Ideal by imparting to the image his total comprehension of the inherent 'qualities and causes' of natural forces, and his sense of a metaphysical energy underlying those dynamics.

In the far distance and partially masked by the snowstorm is the Mont Blanc massif, while before it is the avalanche spilling down to the valley floor. Whirling around and framing everything in its vortical sweep is the raincloud that is responsible for the inundation. The river surges wildly towards the bottom-left where someone drowns in its waters. Another drowned individual is lifted onto the river-bank at the bottom-right where the people look especially doll-like, again pointing up Turner's lifelong and wholly conscious desire to make us look as much as possible like manipulable, pathetic objects when confronted by the terrifying powers of the external world.

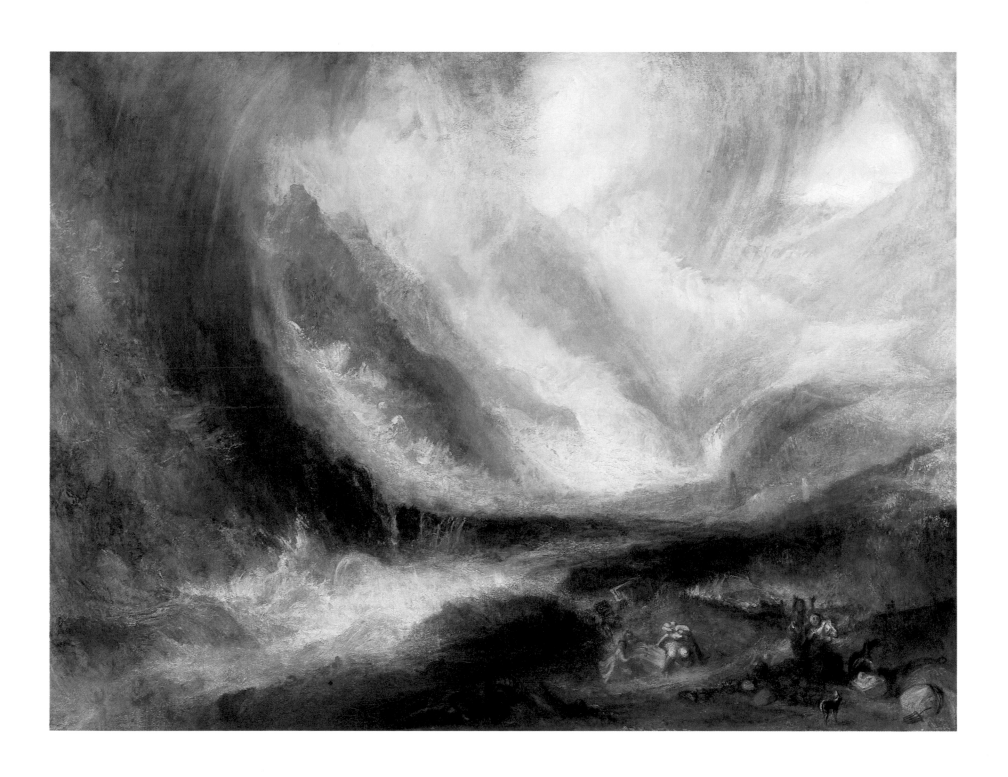

Modern Italy — The Pifferari, 1838

92.5 × 123 cm. Glasgow Art Gallery and Museum

This is one of a pair of paintings exhibited at the Royal Academy in 1838, its pendant being *Ancient Italy — Ovid banished from Rome*, which is now in an American private collection. The *pifferari* are musicians from the Abruzzi, a mountainous region south of Rome, who in order to ease the labour pains of the Virgin wander down to Rome and other central Italian cities before Christmas to play their *pifferi* or shawms, double-reeded woodwind instruments, one of which is visible near the bottom-left of this painting, immediately beyond the woman kneeling in prayer. The juxtaposition of the woman and the *pifferari* makes it clear that Turner knew of the religious purpose of such pipers, as does his request, when this painting was subsequently being copied by an engraver, that a child in swaddling clothes and a bird's nest with eggs should be added to the image in order to 'increase the sentiment of the whole'. And by linking the *pifferari* to contemporary prayer Turner was also probably addressing the survival of pagan practices into modern times as well.

In *Ancient Italy — Ovid banished from Rome*, Turner set the banishment of the great poet amid vast buildings and the glaring light of sunset, a timing which clearly prefigures the decline of Rome itself and one that makes it likely that we are looking at an opposed, morning scene here. Turner clearly synthesized this landscape 'from the various draughts which he had made from various scenes and prospects', as recommended by Reynolds (from whom this quotation is taken), although in parts it closely resembles the town and environs of Tivoli, near Rome, a place Turner had frequently painted. With its mountains, procession of monks on the right and *pifferari*, this picture has much in common with the *Harold in Italy* symphony of Turner's contemporary, Hector Berlioz, who drew his overall title from Byron's *Childe Harold's Pilgrimage* but who based the work (with its evocations of mountains in the first movement, religious procession in the second and *pifferari* in the third) upon his experiences of the landscapes and peoples around Rome, just as Turner had done here. It seems unlikely that Turner ever heard the Berlioz (which was written in 1834 and premiered that same year in Paris), but obviously the shared experiences of the two artists shaped their similar imagery.

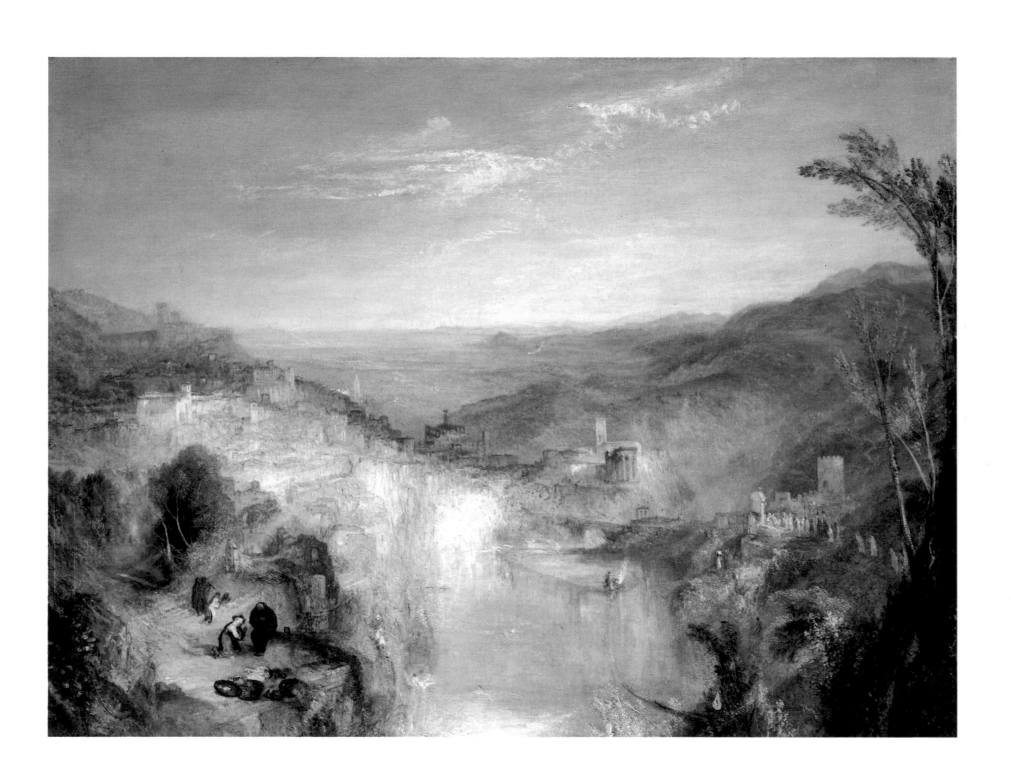

The Fighting 'Temeraire', tugged to her Last Berth to be broken up, 1838, Exh. 1839

91 × 122 cm. National Gallery, London

When this painting was exhibited at the Royal Academy in 1839 its title was accompanied in the catalogue by these lines from Thomas Campbell's 'Ye Mariners of England':

The flag which braved the battle and the breeze,
No longer owns her.

Clearly, Turner felt that cash was beginning to take precedence over national pride, for although the *Téméraire* had fought at the Battle of Trafalgar in 1805, such a noble consideration did not prevent its destruction.

Turner was seen on board a Margate steamer sketching the passage of the *Téméraire* upriver to Beatson's shipbreaking yard at Rotherhithe on 6 September 1838, although what he saw and what he painted are two different things. Thus we know from contemporary newspaper reports that the *Téméraire* was towed by two tugs, and another observer of the towing later testified that the painter invented the spectacular sunset. Moreover, in 1839 Turner was criticized for having transposed the foremast and funnel of the tug, so that the funnel — which should be placed over the tug's engine, midway between its paddles — is now at the prow of the vessel. (That Turner certainly did know the correct order of mast and funnel on a steamer can be seen in the *Dover Castle* of 1822 discussed above.)

He also altered the *Téméraire*. It is certain that a few years earlier she had no yards — the cross-masts from which the sails were hung — and indeed, when she was towed upriver in 1838 she had had all her masts removed, for it was a rule of the Royal Navy that anything salvable from a ship should be taken off her before she was taken away for destruction. And Turner also compressed the scene topographically, so that we are looking eastwards towards the Thames estuary on the left, and westwards towards London on the right. The painter frequently altered topography in such ways.

Yet it is easy to see why he made these changes. The funnel was placed at the prow of the tug so that it appears in the vanguard of all the wind-powered shipping in the picture and therefore symbolizes the 'prophetic idea of smoke, soot, iron and steam, coming to the fore in all naval matters', while the need to create that vanguard explains the appearance of just one tug. The *Téméraire* has had all her masts and sails restored to denote what she had been in her heyday, and she glides *above*, rather than in the water, somewhat like a ghost ship, her disembodied appearance being heightened by the dark tones of the tug which throw her delicate tonalities into relief. And in one of Turner's loveliest matchings of timing to dramatic subject, we see the day coming to its end, just as the *Téméraire* approaches its end, with a moonrise signifying the proximity of night. In the case of the doomed vessel that night will be a long one.

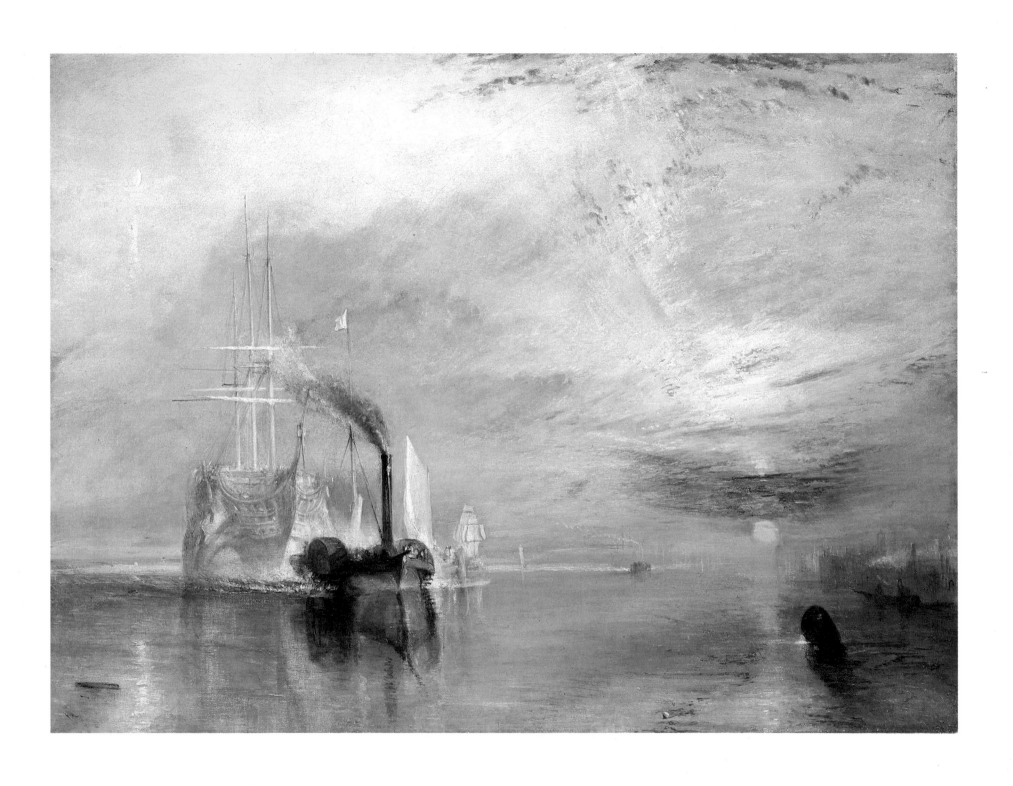

Ancient Rome: Agrippina landing with the Ashes of Germanicus. The Triumphal Bridge and Palace of the Caesars restored, 1839

91.5 × 122 cm. Clore Gallery for the Turner Collection, London

This painting was exhibited in 1839 at the Royal Academy, along with a pendant entitled *Modern Rome — Campo Vaccino* (which is now in a British private collection). Its title was accompanied by these lines in the catalogue:

————The clear stream,

Aye, — the yellow Tiber glimmers to her beam,

Even while the sun is setting.

This verse may be interpreted to mean that we are seeing the last golden blaze of day before the coming of night, and such a light-effect links metaphorically to the subject.

Germanicus Julius Caesar was the adopted son and heir of the Emperor Tiberius, and Turner obtained the account of his death in AD 19 from *The Roman History* by Oliver Goldsmith which was in his library. Goldsmith makes it clear that at the beginning of Tiberius's reign 'nothing appeared [in the Emperor] but prudence, generosity and clemency', but gradually he became madly jealous of Germanicus, the successes of whom 'first brought [Tiberius's] natural disposition to light, and discovered the malignity of his mind without disguise'. Eventually Tiberius had Germanicus poisoned, and Goldsmith tells us that the effects on the Emperor were disastrous, for 'Hitherto Tiberius had kept within bounds . . . But now, from the ninth year of his reign, it is that historians begin to trace the bloody effects of his suspicious temper . . . Having now no object of jealousy to keep him in awe, he began to pull off the mask, and appeared more in his natural character than before.'

Clearly for Turner, as for Goldsmith, the death of Germanicus therefore marked the historical moment at which Rome turned from its golden past to its sad future, for by unbridling the behaviour of Tiberius his demise set Rome on its gradual path to destruction, Tiberius being followed in turn by three more 'mad' Caesars, Caligula, Claudius and Nero. In such a context the last golden blaze of day and the coming of night can only prefigure the death of Rome, just as in the companion painting a lovely twilight complements a contemporary view of the Roman forum in ruins.

A scythe placed at the bottom-right introduces relevant associations of death. In reality the remains of Germanicus, who had died in Antioch, Syria, were landed in Brindisi, not in Rome, but Turner followed Goldsmith in this error. Visually the painting is a magnificent exercise in historical reconstruction, for which Turner drew both upon the influence of Piranesi's similar reconstructions of classical Rome, and upon those of his contemporaries C.R. Cockerall and J.M. Gandy. And it is also a magically coloured picture, being one of those late Turners whose colour still enjoys a matchless richness and beauty.

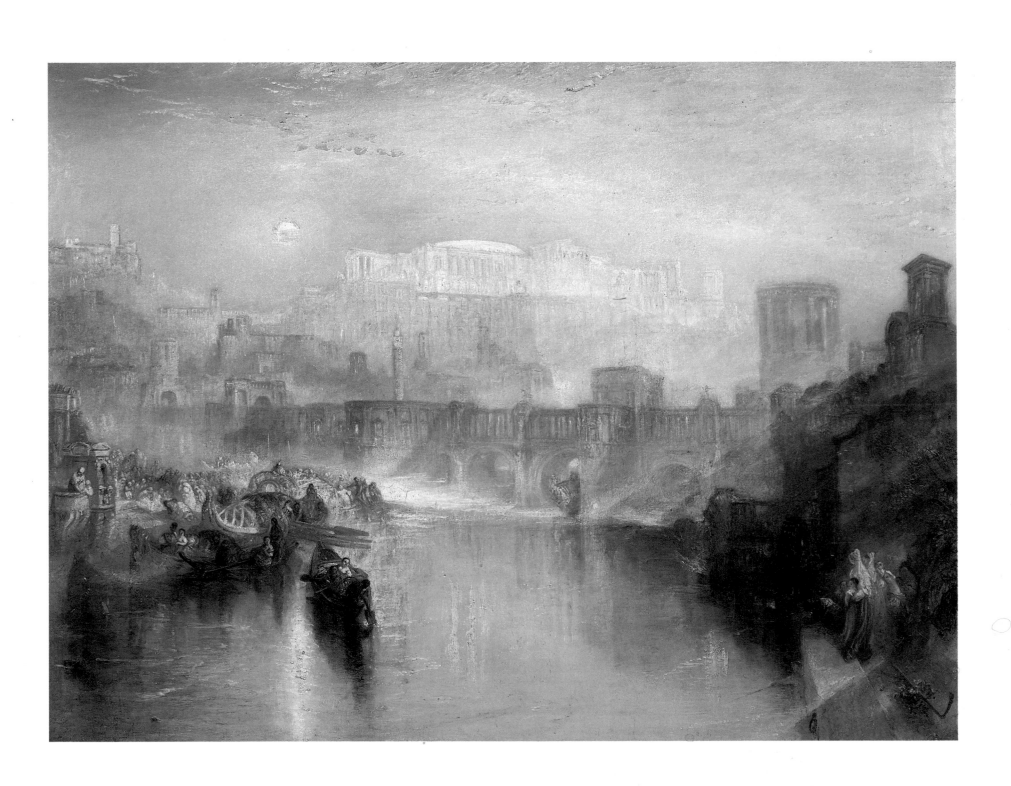

Venice: A storm in the Piazzetta, c. 1840

21.9 × 32.1 cm. National Gallery of Scotland, Edinburgh

Turner visited Venice again in 1840 and this watercolour was apparently made then or soon afterwards. In common with all of his other late Venetian watercolours it was never exhibited during the painter's lifetime.

The whole image takes its cue from the lightning, for the outline of the top of the Doge's Palace blurs into the blue sky beyond and this lack of definition strongly helps communicate the intense electrical energy running through the Piazzetta as lightning flashes across it. On the piazza, too, the blurred shapes of the people add to the sense of urgency as they lift their umbrellas or scurry to escape the lightning. Turner was at his very greatest as a tonalist in this work, for many of the architectural details of the Doge's Palace, and the whole of the visible part of St Mark's Cathedral (seen in the distance beyond the nearby column of St Theodore) were painted in white over a yellow-grey wash that is only slightly darker in tone, although they remain wholly distinctive visually. And at the left, Turner the master of architectural perspectives (and the ex-Professor of Perspective at the Royal Academy) has swung the arcade below the Sansovino Library around so as to present us both with a view down its entire length and also to open out the Piazzetta before it, a fanning-out that is subtly reinforced by the diagonal lines of shadow in the centre-foreground and to the right.

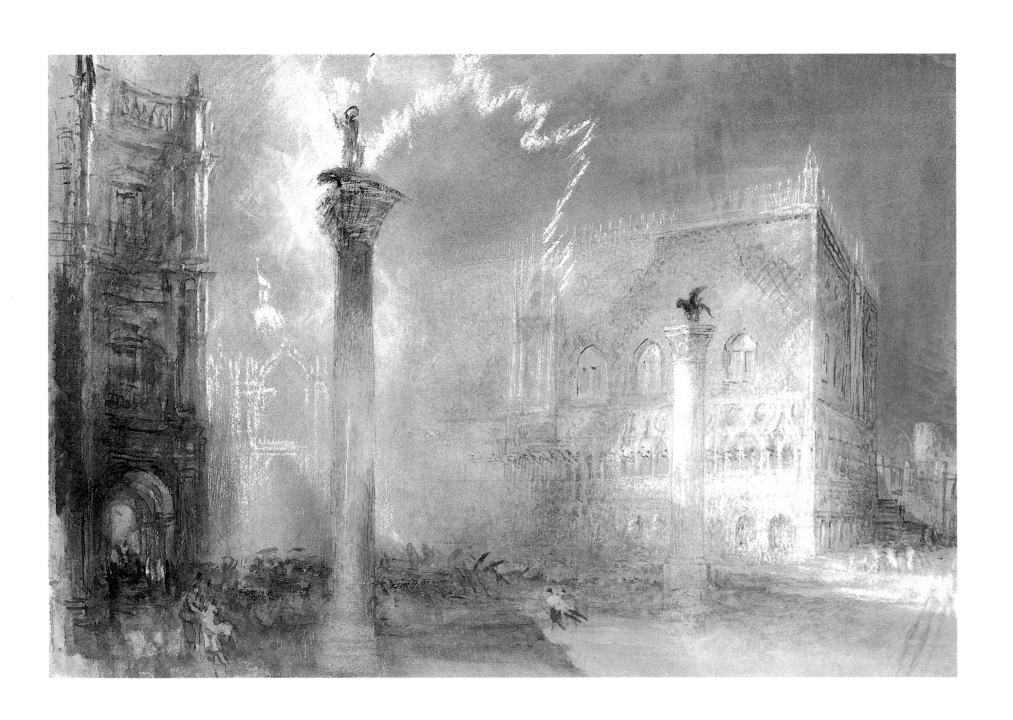

Slavers throwing overboard the Dead and Dying — Typhon coming on, 1840

91 × 138 cm. Museum of Fine Arts, Boston

This painting was exhibited at the Royal Academy in 1840 and it took its subject from Thomas Clarkson's *History . . . of the Abolition of the African Slave Trade by the British Parliament* which had been republished in 1839. Clarkson recounts a court case heard in 1783 in which a group of insurance underwriters sued their clients, the owners and the captain of the slave ship *Zong*, for attempting to defraud them, the owners of the vessel being able to claim for loss of slaves by drowning but not if they died of illness on board ship. When many of the slaves had become ill on a recent voyage, fifty-four of them were immediately thrown overboard, and a further forty-two followed them to a gruesome death on the next day, while over the following three days twenty-six more victims were also put to death, ten of whom 'would not suffer the officers to touch them, but leaped after their companions and shared their fate'. In mitigation, the captain offered the excuse that the action had been necessitated by the fact that there were only two hundred gallons of water on board, and that having missed his last port of call he had no means of replenishing the supply. However, it then emerged that the available supply had not been rationed, and that in any case 'a shower of rain fell and continued for three days immediately after the second lot of slaves had been destroyed, by means of which they might have filled many of their vessels with water and thus prevented all necessity for the destruction of the third' group of slaves. The underwriters won their case but although the Government and the Admiralty were advised of the crime they took no action.

In his title Turner changed the 'shower of rain' into a 'Typhon', and he also added these lines from the 'Fallacies of Hope' to the picture title in the exhibition catalogue:

Aloft all hands, strike the top-masts and belay;
Yon angry setting sun and fierce-edged clouds
Declare the Typhon's coming.
Before it sweeps your decks, throw overboard
The dead and dying — ne'er heed their chains
Hope, Hope, fallacious Hope!
Where is thy market now?

Ultimately the painting comments on how the cash-nexus is the cause of man's inhumanity to man, for here the word 'Hope' signifies merely the hope of profit. In the distance the slave ship has all her sails furled against the approaching 'typhon', while in front of the sanguine sunset (whose associations with blood were clearly intentional) numerous manacled slaves drown as weird and exotic fish dine on their flesh. John Ruskin was the first owner of this painting, and he wrote eloquently about it in *Modern Painters*, but ultimately he was forced to sell it because he was unable to live with its tragic subject.

122

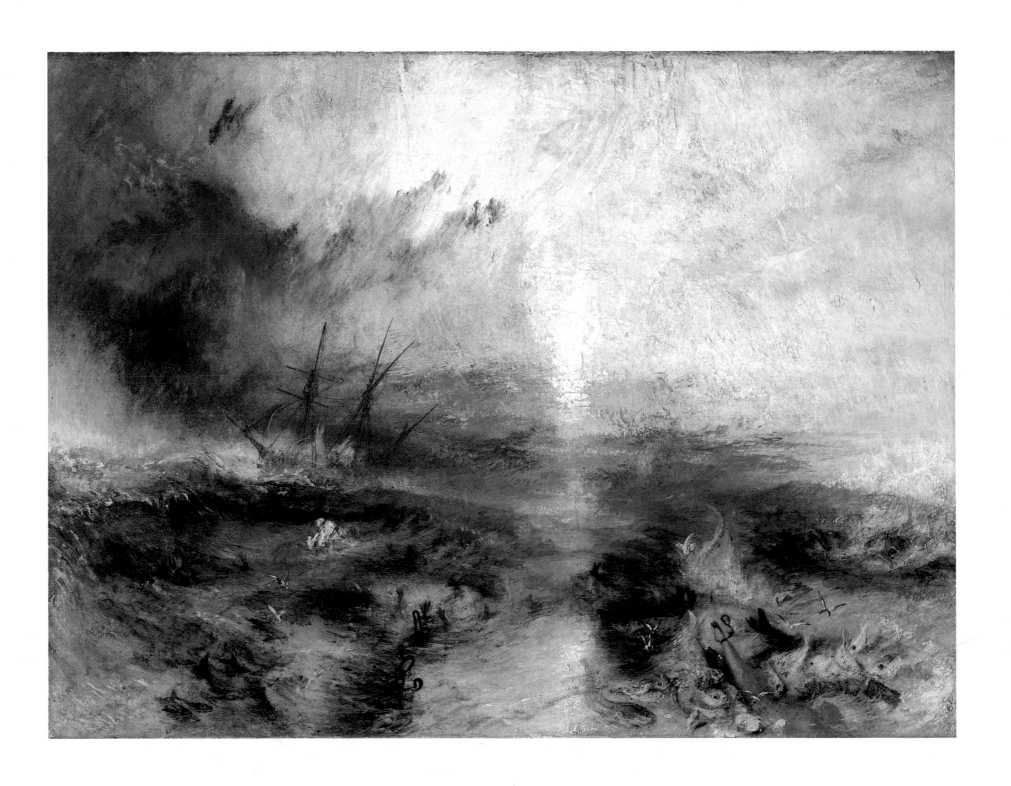

Snow Storm — Steam-Boat off a Harbour's Mouth making Signals in Shallow Water, and going by the Lead. The Author was in this Storm on the Night the Ariel left Harwich, 1842

91.5 × 122 cm. Clore Gallery for the Turner Collection, London

This is perhaps Turner's finest seascape, and indeed possibly the greatest depiction of a storm in all art. It was exhibited at the Royal Academy in 1842.

Turner once claimed that in order to paint this scene he had 'got the sailors to lash me to the mast to observe it; I was lashed for four hours, and I did not expect to escape, but I felt bound to record it if I did'. However, possibly he fabricated this story, for it is similar to one told of the marine painter Joseph Vernet, and no ship named the *Ariel* is known to have sailed from Harwich in the years leading up to 1842; perhaps the title of the vessel was intended to allude to Shakespeare's *The Tempest*. Nor does the picture-title accord fully with what we actually see, for the ship is 'going by the lead', which denotes that a weighted line is being periodically dropped from the bow to gauge the shallowness of the waters so as to prevent the ship from running aground. Yet such a prudent, measured precaution seems to be at odds with the actual predicament of a vessel caught up in a maelstrom, even if we can appreciate why the boat should be firing signal rockets to denote her position offshore.

Yet even if some or all of Turner's factual claims are false, and there seems to be some disparity between the nautical behaviour indicated in the title and what appears to be actually happening to the *Ariel*, the veracity of Turner's communication of what it is like to be at the centre of a cataclysmic storm is beyond dispute, with the entire visible universe wheeling in a massive vortex around both the steamer and also the spectator. (And on the steamer, incidentally, we can see that its foremast and funnel are located in the correct positions, which again indicates that Turner had purposefully taken liberties with literal reality in *The Fighting 'Temeraire'* of three years earlier.)

Turner was very vexed by reading a criticism of this work that it represents a mass of 'soapsuds and whitewash', and was overheard to say 'soapsuds and whitewash! What would they have? I wonder what they think the sea's like? I wish they'd been in it.' But today it is easier to appreciate that his freedom of handling imparts the raw energy of a storm far more authentically than if he had painted every drop of rain or every wave in the sea with greater degrees of verisimilitude.

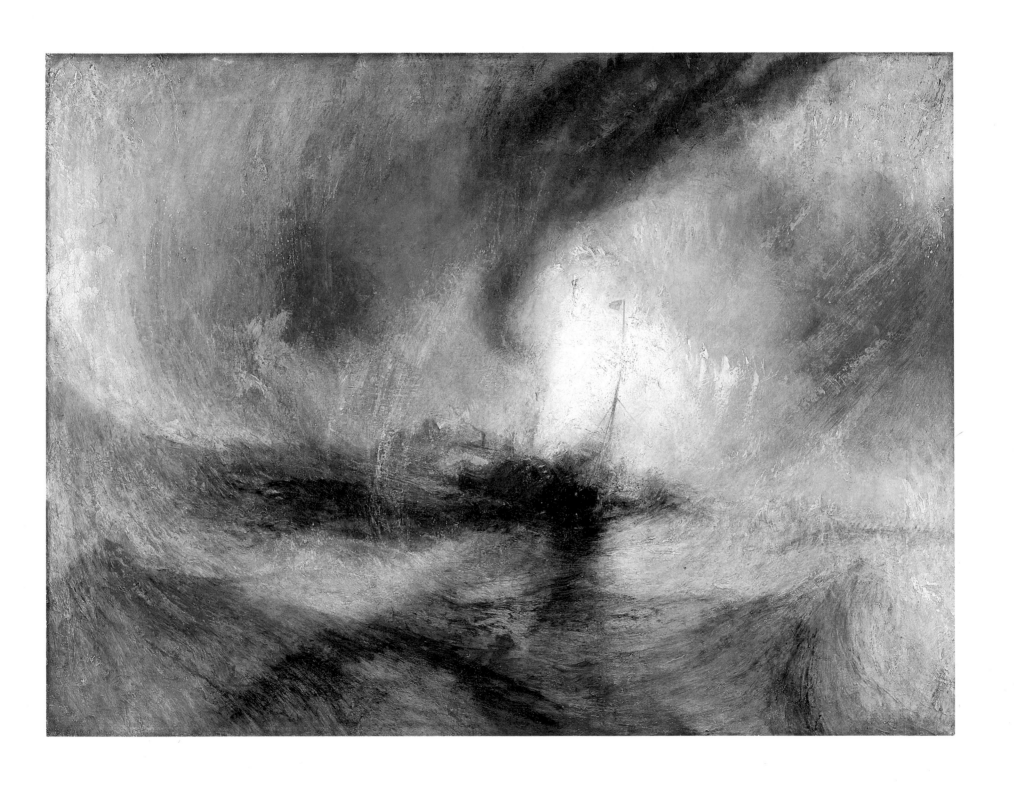

Rain, Steam and Speed — the Great Western Railway, 1844

91 × 122 cm. National Gallery, London

When this painting was first exhibited at the Royal Academy in 1844 the anonymous critic of *Fraser's Magazine* warned its readers to hasten to see the work lest the train 'should dash out of the picture, and be away up Charing Cross through the wall opposite'. That warning does not seem untoward, given that the train does communicate an immense sense of velocity. Principally such movement is imparted by the enforced perspective of the railway line and bridge which appear dramatically out of the distant haze of rain, but originally it was also assisted by three puffs of steam emanating from the locomotive which have been 'already left behind by the engine'. These puffs are now scarcely visible but they were remembered in 1857 as having originally been much more distinct, and thus contributing greatly to furthering the sense of speed in the train. And Turner also joked about speed here, for in front of the engine is a hare who may or may not be outpacing it. Because of the pictorial proximity of the animal to a distant ploughman beyond the bridge, it seems certain that the painter intended the conjunction of fast hare and slow plough to remind his audience of the popular song 'Speed the plough', a ditty he is known to have been acquainted with. The bridge itself has been identified as Brunel's railway bridge over the Thames at Maidenhead, with the older bridge carrying the Great West Road visible on the left.

In addition to the 'Speed' of the title and the 'Rain' falling across the entire scene, we can also perceive the 'Steam', for Turner has removed the front of the locomotive in order to show us the inner workings of its boiler. Nothing else would explain the brilliant fiery mass at the front of the train, for it is too formless to be an outside light. Instead, and once again, we are witnessing a realization of Turner's desire to make visible the underlying 'causes' of things, albeit directly rather than covertly.

Turner himself owned shares in the Great Western Railway Company, and so he may have had a secondary and surreptitious reason for exalting the power of Steam in this picture. But in any case, he had already celebrated the coming of Steam long before, as we have already noted in the *Dover Castle* of 1822. And if in *The Fighting 'Temeraire'* of 1839 he equally regretted the advent of Steam, that merely indicates his ambivalence towards the Industrial Revolution.

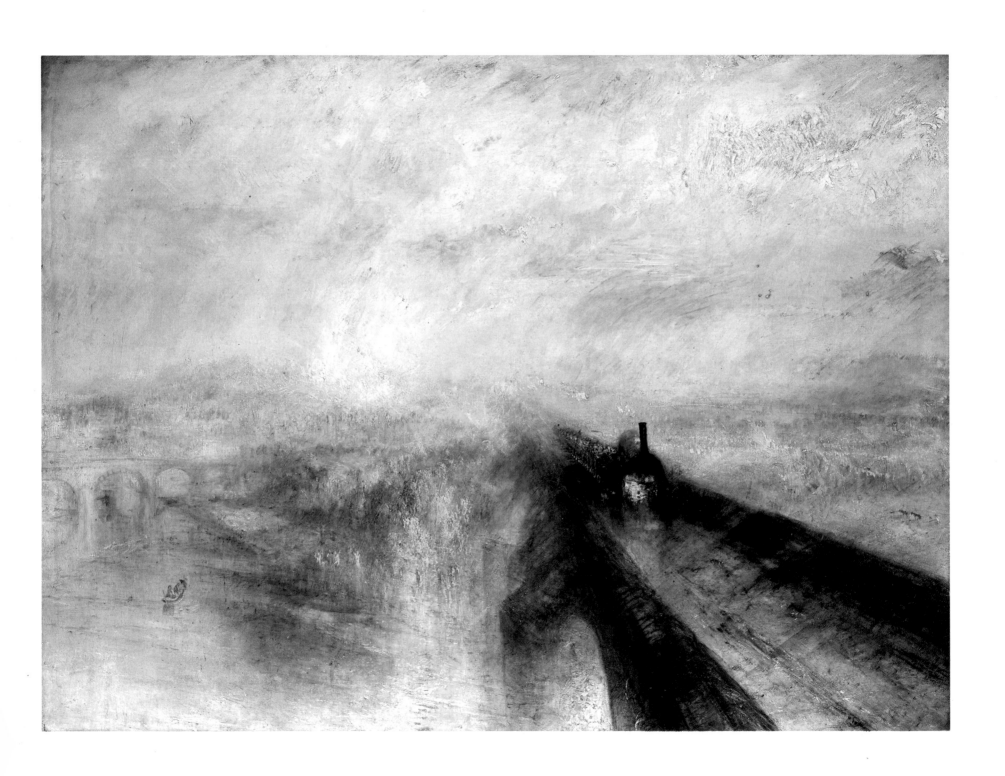

Lake Lucerne: the Bay of Uri from above Brunnen, 1842

29.8 × 45.7 cm. Private Collection

In the early 1840s Switzerland took on a new appeal for Turner and he visited it each summer between 1841 and 1844. There he made a great number of sketches and broadly washed watercolours, some of which served as the basis of more highly finished designs. In London he had several of the broad watercolours shown to prospective clients with a view to obtaining commissions for further highly finished designs to be made from them, along with four of the highly finished watercolours themselves (of which this drawing was one). Eventually there would be four sets of more elaborate watercolours, although not all of the works were made on commission as Turner's patrons found the painter's late style somewhat difficult to understand. The present watercolour was itself based upon a broad sample-study still in the Turner Bequest in London.

Turner loved Lake Lucerne, and especially the lower part known as the Urnersee, or Bay of Uri, which we view here from above the small town of Brunnen. In addition to a good number of rough portrayals of the lake around Brunnen, between 1841 and 1845 Turner also made three highly finished watercolours of this same panorama, while a fourth drawing represents the view looking off to the right in a westerly direction along the main body of the lake.

In the distance on the left and jutting out into the lake is the Tellsplatte promontory, at the base of which stands William Tell's chapel; opposite, on the right, is the immense Uri-Rotstock mountain (9606 ft/2928 m). Before it are the lower peaks of the Oberbauenstock glinting in gold above the great mass of the Seelisberg promontory and the Rütli meadow, a hallowed spot in Swiss history. However, historical associations do not seem to have interested the painter here, for faced with scenery like this, the ancient affairs of men were no longer of much consequence. Only the present, humble doings of mankind interested Turner in these settings, and then usually just to establish the scale of their vast surroundings.

The composition is unified by the great sweep up into the rainclouds rising above the Tellsplatte promontory, and by the matching line of shadow passing across the Oberbauenstock on the far side of the lake. This expansive framing device sets off the more distant mountain ranges that seemingly float in the misty, early morning light. Both on the mountains and on the lake itself we can witness Turner's widespread use of stippling, equally to denote the multitude of trees and their reflections, and to add a sense of vibrancy to the scene, almost making it shimmer. And Turner's interlinked powers as a colourist and tonalist can be witnessed to the full here, for although the colours of the Uri-Rotstock and the more distant mountains are beautifully soft and pearly, the tangibility of those mountains is never in doubt, being effected by incredibly delicate modulations of tone.

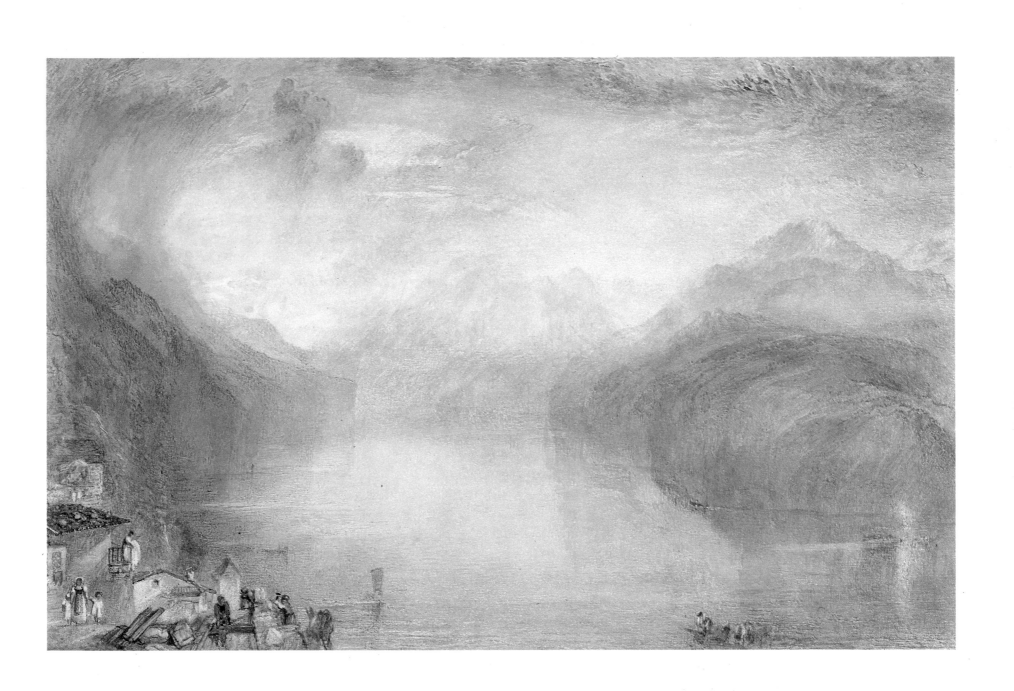

The Lake of Geneva with the Dent d'Oche: tending the vines, 1841

22.8 × 29.1 cm. Clore Gallery for the Turner Collection, London

On several of Turner's later tours he used sketchbooks with limp covers that could be rolled up and were thus very portable. The present watercolour was made in one such roll sketchbook, the *Fribourg, Lausanne and Geneva* sketchbook in which, as the title implies, the majority of identifiable studies represent towns around and to the north of Lake Geneva.

To the east of Lausanne the hillsides around Lutry support extensive vineyards, and from them one obtains superb views across Lake Geneva towards the Dent d'Oche massif on the south side of the lake. Turner made a sequence of four watercolours of this panorama across two different sketchbooks, the *Fribourg, Lausanne and Geneva* sketchbook and the *Lausanne* sketchbook that was also in use on the 1841 Swiss tour. These watercolours were evidently created from memory and the imagination, for although the relative position of the lake and distant mountains remains constant in each, the types of activity in the foreground and the foregrounds themselves differ from drawing to drawing — obviously the artist was creating variations on a theme. Thus in one watercolour we see a funeral procession making its way towards a cemetery, and in another we can perceive the same cemetery but from a closer viewpoint. Here, however, Turner portrayed the vineyards and grapepickers that he would have witnessed in reality.

In the distance the huge massif rises above the lake amid a haze of gorgeous colour, Turner having washed his paint onto wet paper and allowed it to diffuse before adding the foreground details after the paper had dried. But clearly he found the very lack of definition in his forms highly expressive here, for he did not elaborate the distant mountains at all, and his decision not to do so is not surprising, given the unearthly beauty of their colour.

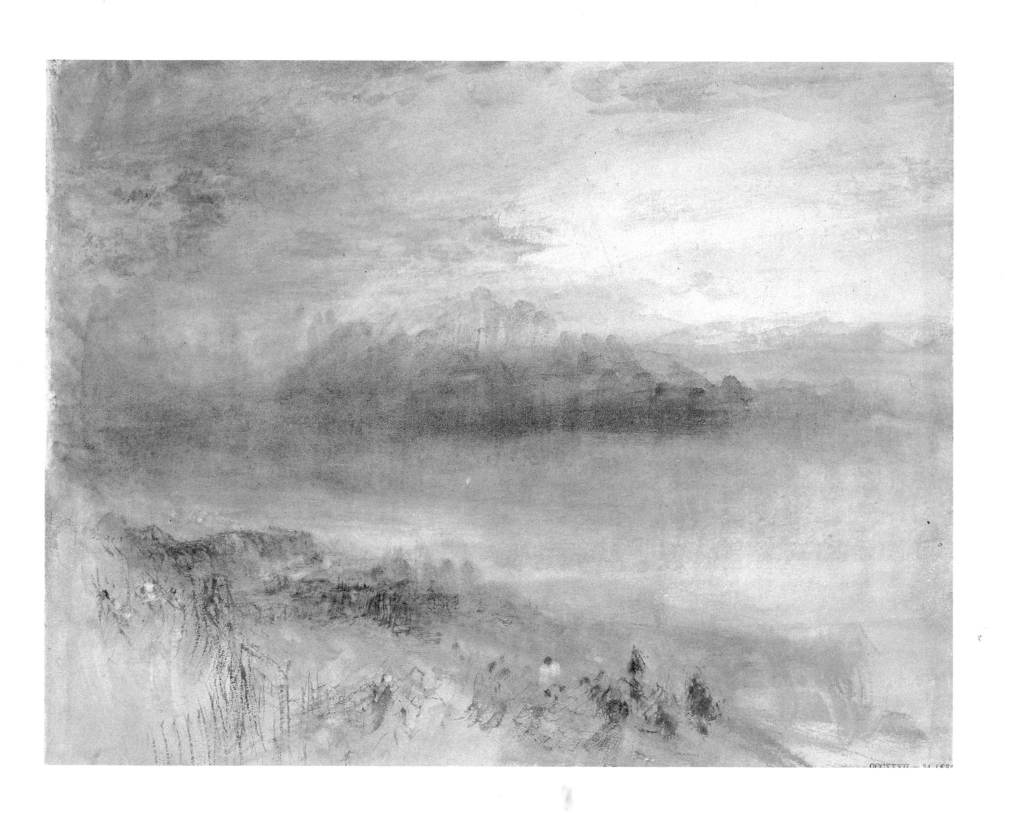

Montreux, c. 1841

23.4 × 33 cm. Clore Gallery for the Turner Collection, London

The subject of this watercolour has not previously been identified (indeed, it is listed in the inventory of the Turner Bequest simply as 'Water Colour') and it is a page from yet another of the roll sketchbooks used on the Swiss tour of 1841. That book was itself later given the title of the *Lausanne* sketchbook because thirteen of the sixteen watercolours contained in it clearly show views in or around Lausanne, on the north side of Lake Geneva.

To the east of Lausanne the shores of Lake Geneva gradually swing around southwards to Montreux and the Rhône valley leading down to Martigny; here we look southwards at sunset across to Montreux, with the shadow of one of the lower peaks of the Dent d'Oche range, the Le Grammont mountain (7125 ft/2157 m), on the right. (On the opposite side of the Rhône valley Turner has just indicated the bases of the mountains.) In the foreground the dark tones of a small wooded island and a watermill lend an immense sense of depth to the landscape beyond. Turner has washed his colour very freely here, and the opalescent pinks and pale blue-greys in the distance make this one of his loveliest unfinished drawings.

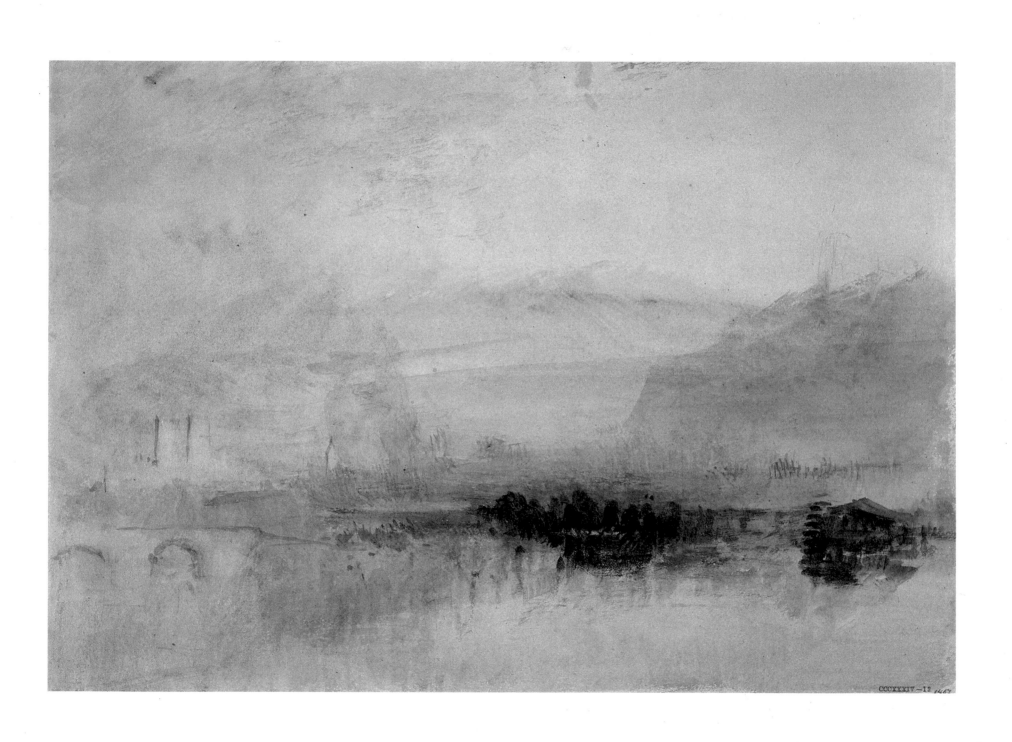

The Devil's Bridge, St Gotthard, c. 1843

23.8 × 30.5 cm. Fitzwilliam Museum, Cambridge

The St Gotthard Pass, to the south of Andermatt in the Canton of Uri, is one of the major routes through the Swiss alps into Italy, and the painter had depicted the so-called Devil's Bridge across the pass several times after making his first tour of Switzerland in 1802. In all of those earlier works he used an upright format to enhance the vast sense of scale in the landscape, whereas here he employed his more usual horizontal format to establish the immensity of the landscape. He also located the bridge more distantly than he had done in the earlier works so that it is dominated by its surroundings, and it is easy to see why he did so, for amid all the brutal grandeur of this scenery the creations of man appear very puny indeed.

As in many of the other late Swiss watercolours, there is a sense of energy running through the inert masses of rock, so that the whole visible realm seems possessed by movement. Yet this sense of movement was not just a painterly fancy on Turner's part; we know from the artist's own writings that he believed in a metaphysical reality underlying appearances, and in his late works he arrived at a superb synthesis of style and content, for the constantly varied modulations of tone act simultaneously as expressive devices, as means of communicating Turner's knowledge of the 'truths' of geological form, as statements of the natural energies swirling around the alps, as realizations of those primal energies that brought the rocks into being, and ultimately as a means of communicating Turner's apprehension of the divine continuum pulsing through everything.

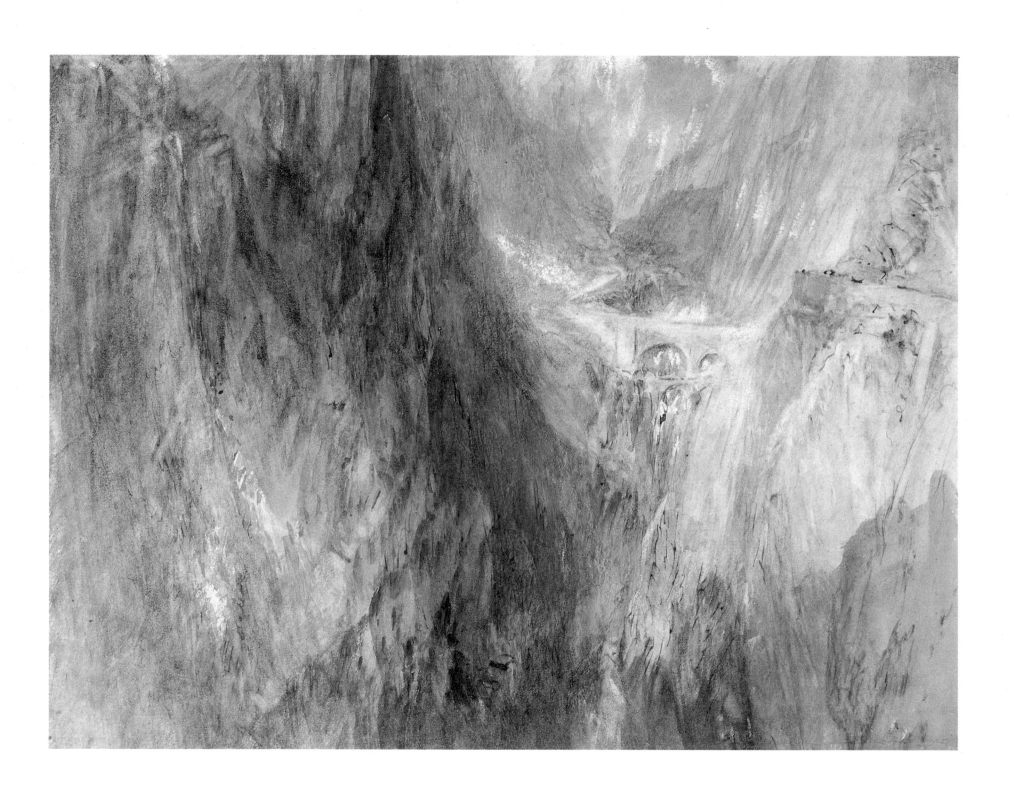

The Falls of the Clyde, c. 1844–1846

89 × 119.5 cm. Lady Lever Art Gallery, Port Sunlight

This is one of a superb group of late paintings in which Turner reworked subjects he had used earlier in the 'Liber Studiorum' set of prints made between 1806 and the early 1820s. The present picture was based upon Plate 18 of the 'Liber Studiorum', published in 1809, a design that itself derived from a sepia watercolour made a year or so earlier. Turner had kept in his possession all the mezzotint printing plates of the 'Liber Studiorum', and in 1845 he had all those prints run off again, even though the plates were very worn. Possibly that reprinting acted as a stimulus for the late set of paintings.

The Cora Linn waterfall is one of three waterfalls on the river Clyde south of Glasgow, and Turner had first depicted it in a watercolour he exhibited at the Royal Academy in 1802 (the sepia watercolour made for the 'Liber Studiorum' was developed from that earlier design). In the title of the 1802 watercolour in the exhibition catalogue, Turner referred the viewer to Mark Akenside's poem 'Hymn to the Naiads', both to explain that the women in his foreground were not ordinary ladies improbably bathing naked in the cold waters of the river Clyde, and simultaneously to make clear his identification with the concept Akenside had elaborated in his poem, namely that the underlying forces of nature were personified by the Naiads or river nymphs. Even in 1802 Turner was attempting to articulate the universals behind appearances. Although by that time he had fully mastered the fundamentals of hydrodynamic motion, and of architectural and geological forms, nonetheless clearly he felt that if he wanted to be absolutely specific about portraying universals, it would do no harm to enlist the aid of symbols such as Akenside's Naiads. But by the mid-1840s, when he painted this picture, he no longer had any need of symbols, for by then he had attained such immense powers over form and colour that they allowed him to state with the utmost subtlety the primal energies earlier symbolized by the river nymphs. Indeed, those women-deities are here barely perceptible, for the energies they personify now flow through the entire landscape itself.

The Falls of the Clyde is also one of Turner's very greatest masterworks in terms of its colour, being equally a study of the way that strong light breaks down prismatically as it passes through the fine spray of moisture given off by a waterfall. Here Turner brought together all his lifelong concerns, with form, meaning, colour and optics, in a paean to the forces of nature and art.

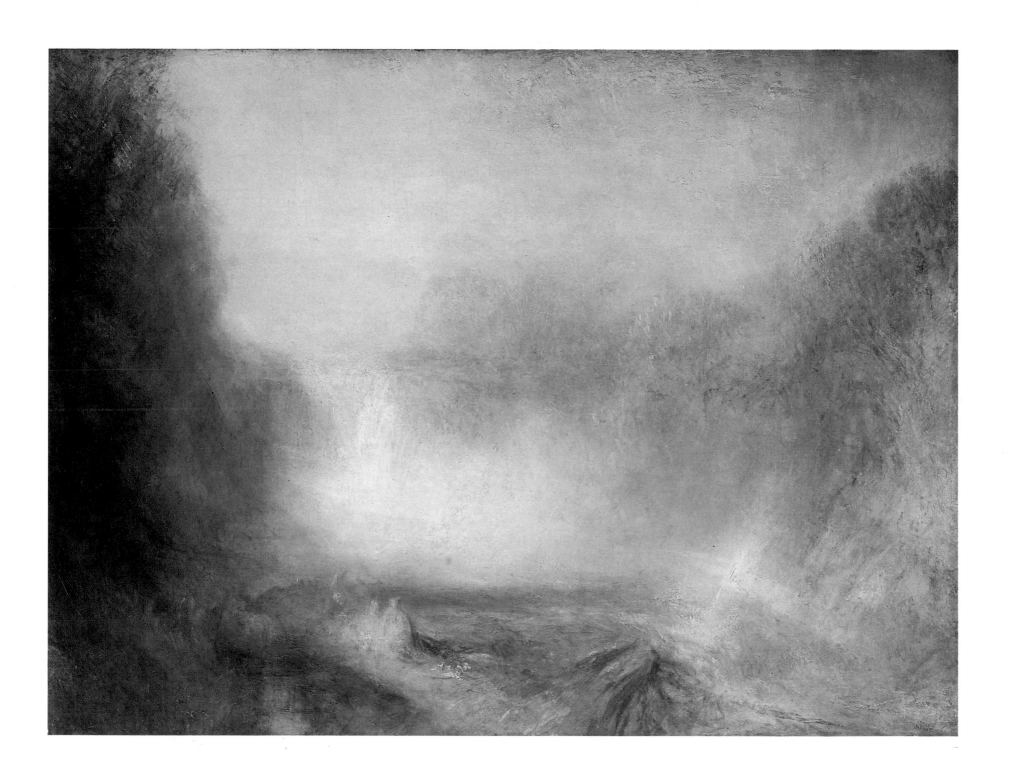

Yacht approaching the Coast, c. 1845–1850

102 × 142 cm. Clore Gallery for the Turner Collection, London

The title of this work is not Turner's own, for he never exhibited it. Its date is equally uncertain, although the boldness of the paint handling does suggest that it could have been made as late as 1850, for the area of thick scumbled paint around the sun and the drawing of the yacht are identical with the way that the sun and ancillary forms are painted in the pictures that Turner exhibited at the Royal Academy in 1850. A further link between this painting and Turner's other last exhibited works is the centrality of the sun in the image.

For this is surely not just a picture of a yacht approaching a coast: it is Turner's great hymn to the sun, that orb that he is reputed to have said is God. The painter's lifelong identification with poetry that linked the power of light to the Divinity, his open identification with the Platonic metaphysics of Mark Akenside, his constant concern with essentials — of natural process, of human behaviour and of the mechanics of light and form — all these factors equally point to his belief that the sun is not merely a physical object. And naturally his paintings perhaps best make that identification clear, for in works such as this Turner's sun burns its way into the heavens as the ultimate source of all life on earth, the key to all those other essentials that he had spent a lifetime exploring and celebrating.

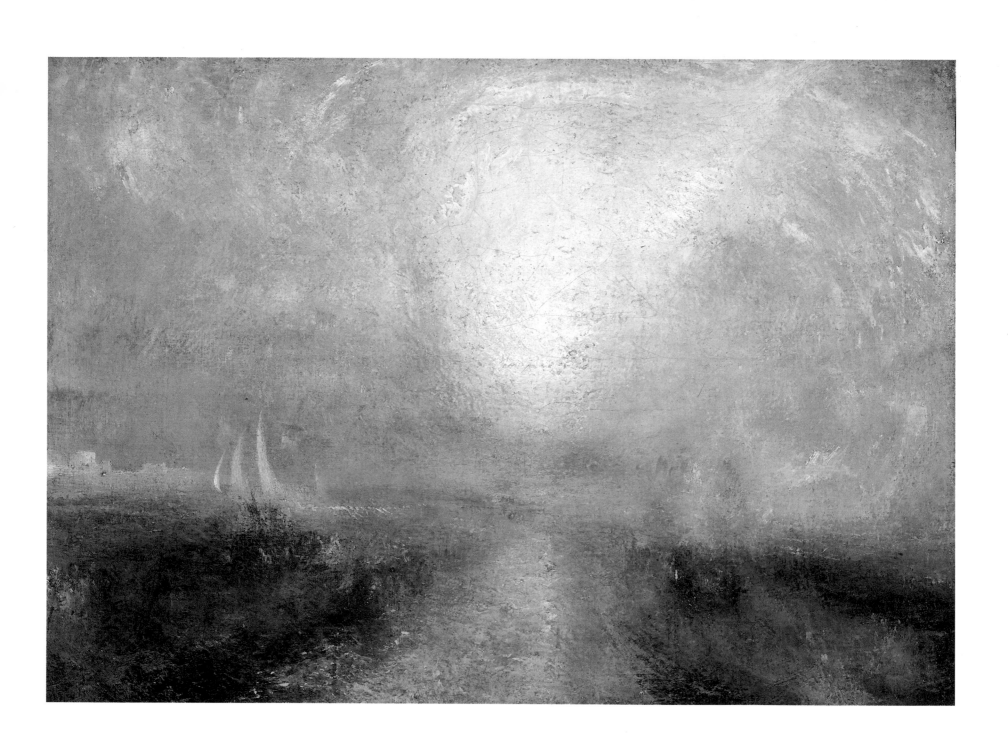

SELECTED BIBLIOGRAPHY

BUTLIN, Martin and JOLL, Evelyn, *The Paintings of J.M.W. Turner*, Rev. ed., 2 Vols., London, 1984.

FINBERG, A.J., *The Life of J.M.W. Turner, R.A.*, 2nd ed., London, 1961.

——*A Complete Inventory of the Drawings in the Turner Bequest*, 2 Vols., London, 1909.

GAGE, John, *Colour in Turner: Poetry and Truth*, London, 1969.

——*J.M.W. Turner, 'A Wonderful Range of Mind'*, London, 1987.

HILL, David, *In Turner's Footsteps*, London, 1984.

LINDSAY, Jack, *J.M.W. Turner, His Life and Work. A Critical Biography*, London, 1966.

POWELL, Cecilia, *Turner in the South*, London, 1987.

RAWLINSON, W.G., *The Engraved Work of J.M.W. Turner*, 2 Vols., London, 1908, 1913.

——*Turner's Liber Studiorum, a Description and a Catalogue*, London, 1878, 2nd ed., 1906.

RUSKIN, John, *Modern Painters*, abridged version ed. David Barrie, London, 1987.

SHANES, Eric, *Turner's Picturesque Views in England and Wales*, London, 1979.

——*Turner's Rivers, Harbours and Coasts*, London, 1981.

——*Turner's Human Landscape*, London, 1990.

——*Turner's England*, London, 1990.

TURNER STUDIES, a half-yearly journal published by the Tate Gallery, London.

THORNBURY, Walter, *The Life of J.M.W. Turner*, 2 Vols., London, 1862, 2nd ed., 1877.

WILKINSON, Gerald, *Turner's Early Sketchbooks*, London, 1972.

——*The Sketches of Turner, R.A.*, London, 1974.

——*Turner's Colour Sketches*, London, 1975.

WILTON, Andrew, *The Life and Work of J.M.W. Turner*, London, 1979.

——*Turner in his time*, London, 1987.

CHRONOLOGY

1775
Birth of Joseph Mallord William Turner in London on 23 April (?).
1787
Makes first signed and dated watercolours.
1789
Probably begins studying with Thomas Malton, Jr, and is also admitted as student to Royal Academy Schools.
1790
Exhibits first work at the R.A.
1791
Tours the West Country.
1792
Tours south and central Wales.
1793
Awarded the 'Greater Silver Pallet' for landscape drawing by the Royal Society of Arts.
1794
Tours Midlands and north Wales.
1795
Tours southern England and south Wales.
1796
Exhibits first oil painting at the Royal Academy.
1797
Tours north of England and Lake District.
1798
Tours north Wales.
1799
Elected an Associate Royal Academician. Visits West Country, Lancashire and north Wales. First daughter Evelina born around this time?
1801
Tours Scotland.
1802
Elected Royal Academician. Tours Switzerland. Second daughter Georgiana born around this time?
1804
Death of mother after a long illness.
1805
Holds first exhibition in own gallery in London.
1807
Elected Royal Academy Professor of Perspective.
1808
Visits Cheshire and Wales. Probably pays first visit to Farnley Hall, home of Walter Fawkes.

1811
Delivers first course of perspective lectures at the Royal Academy.
Tours West Country for material for the 'Southern Coast' series.

1812
First quotation from his own poem, 'Fallacies of Hope', in the R.A. catalogue.

1813
Completes Sandycombe Lodge in Twickenham. Revisits West Country.

1814
Again tours West Country?

1815
Tours Yorkshire.

1816
Tours Yorkshire to gain material for the 'Richmondshire' series.

1817
Tours Belgium, Germany and Holland.

1818
Visits Edinburgh.

1819
Walter Fawkes exhibits over sixty of Turner's watercolours in his London residence. Pays first visit to Italy, stays in Venice, Florence, Rome and Naples.

1821
Visits Paris and tours northern France.

1822
Visits Edinburgh for State Visit of King George IV.

1824
Tours south-east England.

1825
Tours Holland, Germany and Belgium. Death of Walter Fawkes.

1826
Tours Germany, Brittany and the Loire. Starts visiting Petworth regularly.

1827
Stays at East Cowes castle, the home of the architect John Nash.

1828
Delivers last lectures as R.A. Professor of Perspective. Visits Italy a second time, stays principally in Rome.

1829
Exhibits seventy-nine 'England and Wales' series watercolours in London. Visits Paris, Normandy and Brittany. Death of father. Draws up first draft of will.

1830
Tours Midlands. Exhibits a watercolour for last time at the Royal Academy.

1831
Tours Scotland. Revises will.

1832
Visits Paris, probably meets Delacroix.

1833
Exhibits more 'England and Wales' watercolours in London. Visits Copenhagen, Berlin, Dresden, Prague, Vienna and Venice.

1834
Tours the Meuse, Moselle and Rhineland.

1835
Possibly tours Germany.

1836
Tours France, Switzerland and the Val d'Aosta.

1837
Death of Lord Egremont. Resigns as R.A. Professor of Perspective.

1840
Meets John Ruskin for first time. Visits Venice.

1841
Tours Switzerland, and does so again in following three summers.

1845
Acts as temporary President of Royal Academy. Tours northern France in May; in the autumn Dieppe and Picardy, his last tour.

1846
Moves to Chelsea around this time.

1848–49
Growing infirmity. Revises will.

1850
Exhibits for last time at the Royal Academy.

1851
Dies 19 December in Chelsea, London.

LIST OF PLATES

5: J.W. Archer, *J.M.W. Turner's birthplace in Maiden Lane, Covent Garden*, 1852, watercolour, British Museum, London.

6: *Self-Portrait, c.* 1798, oil on canvas, 74.5 × 58.5 cm, Clore Gallery for the Turner Collection, London.

7: J.W. Archer, *Attic in Turner's birthplace in Maiden Lane, Covent Garden, said to have been Turner's first studio*, 1852, watercolour, British Museum, London.

9: J.M.W. Turner, *Folly Bridge and Bacon's Tower, Oxford*, 1787, pen and ink with watercolour, 30.8 × 43.2 cm, Clore Gallery for the Turner Collection, London.

10: J.M.W. Turner, *The Pantheon, the morning after the fire*, R.A. 1792, watercolour, 39.5 × 51.5 cm, Clore Gallery for the Turner Collection, London.

11: J.M.W. Turner, *Tom Tower, Oxford, c.* 1793, watercolour, 27.3 × 21.5 cm, Clore Gallery for the Turner Collection, London.

14: J.M.W. Turner, *Dolbadern Castle, North Wales*, R.A. 1800, oil on canvas, 119.5 × 90.2 cm, Royal Academy of Arts, London.

17: J.M.W. Turner, *South view from the cloisters, Salisbury Cathedral, c.* 1802, watercolour, 68 × 49.6 cm, Victoria and Albert Museum, London.

18: J.M.W. Turner, *Mer de Glace, with Blair's Cabin*, 1802, watercolour, 31.5 × 46.8 cm, Clore Gallery for the Turner Collection, London.

19: J.M.W. Turner, *Frontispiece of 'Liber Studiorum'*, mezzotint engraving, 1812.

21: J.M.W. Turner, *Norham Castle on the Tweed*, mezzotint engraving for the 'Liber Studiorum', 1816.

22: William Havell, *Sandycombe Lodge, Twickenham, the Seat of J.M.W. Turner, R.A., c.* 1814, watercolour, 10.8 × 20 cm, Private Collection, U.K.

26: J.M.W. Turner, *Northampton, Northamptonshire*, Winter 1830–31, watercolour on paper, 29 × 44 cm, Private Collection, U.S.A.

28: J.M.W. Turner, *The Field of Waterloo*, R.A. 1818, oil on canvas, 147.5 × 239 cm, Clore Gallery for the Turner Collection, London.

30: J.M.W. Turner, *The Bay of Baiæ: Apollo and the Sybil*, R.A. 1823, oil on canvas, 145.5 × 237.5 cm, Clore Gallery for the Turner Collection, London.

31(l.): W. Radclyffe after J.M.W. Turner, *Deal, Kent*, line engraving on copper made for the 'Picturesque Views on the Southern Coast' series, 1826.

31(r.): J.M.W. Turner, *The Artist and his Admirers, c.* 1827, watercolour on blue paper, 14 × 19 cm, Clore Gallery for the Turner Collection, London.

33: J.M.W. Turner, *Messieurs les voyageurs on their return from Italy (par le diligence) in a snow drift on Mount Tarrar — 22nd of January, 1829*, R.A. 1829, watercolour, 54.5 × 74.7 cm, British Museum, London.

34: J.M.W. Turner, *A scene in the Val d'Aosta, c.* 1836, watercolour, 23.7 × 29.8 cm, Fitzwilliam Museum, Cambridge.

37: William Henry Hunt (?), *Portrait of J.M.W. Turner, c.* 1845, Lady Lever Art Gallery, Port Sunlight, U.K.

38: J.W. Archer, *House of J.M.W. Turner at Chelsea*, 1852, watercolour, British Museum, London.

39: William Parrott, *Turner on Varnishing Day, c.*1846, oil on wood panel, University of Reading, Reading, U.K.

40: Turner's death mask, National Portrait Gallery, London.

42: J.M.W. Turner, *The Departure of the Fleet*, R.A. 1850, oil on canvas, 91.5 × 122 cm, Clore Gallery for the Turner Collection, London.

45: J.M.W. Turner, *The Archbishop's Palace, Lambeth*, R.A. 1790, watercolour, 26.3 × 37.8 cm, Indianapolis Museum of Art, Indianapolis, Indiana, U.S.A.

47: J.M.W. Turner, *St Anselm's Chapel, with part of Thomas-à-Becket's crown, Canterbury Cathedral*, R.A. 1794, watercolour, 51.7 × 37.4 cm, Whitworth Art Gallery, Manchester, U.K.

49: J.M.W. Turner, *Fishermen at Sea*, R.A. 1796, oil on canvas, 91.5 × 122.4 cm, Clore Gallery for the Turner Collection, London.

51: J.M.W. Turner, *Dutch Boats in a Gale: Fishermen endeavouring to put their Fish on Board* ('The Bridgewater Seapiece'), R.A. 1801, oil on canvas, 162.5 × 222 cm, Private Collection, on loan to the National Gallery, London.

53: J.M.W. Turner, *Interior of Salisbury Cathedral, looking towards the North Transept, c.* 1802–5, watercolour, 66 × 50.8 cm, Salisbury and South Wiltshire Museum.

55: J.M.W. Turner, *Calais Pier, with French Poissards preparing for Sea: an English Packet arriving*, R.A. 1803, oil on canvas, 172 × 240 cm, National Gallery, London.

57: J.M.W. Turner, *The Great Fall of the Riechenbach, in the valley of Hasle, Switzerland*, 1804, watercolour, 102.2 × 68.9 cm, Cecil Higgins Art Gallery, Bedford, U.K.

59: J.M.W. Turner, *The Shipwreck*, Turner's Gallery 1805, oil on canvas, 170.5 × 241.5 cm, Clore Gallery for the Turner Collection, London.

61: J.M.W. Turner, *Sun rising through Vapour; Fishermen cleaning and selling Fish*, R.A. 1807, oil on canvas, 134.5 × 179 cm, National Gallery, London.

63: J.M.W. Turner, *Pope's Villa at Twickenham*, Turner's Gallery 1808, oil on canvas, 91.5 × 120.6 cm, Sudeley Castle, Winchcombe, Gloucestershire, U.K.

65: J.M.W. Turner, *Snow Storm: Hannibal and his Army crossing the Alps*, R.A. 1812, oil on canvas, 146 × 237.5 cm, Clore Gallery for the Turner Collection, London.

67: J.M.W. Turner, *Dido building Carthage; or, the Rise of the Carthaginian Empire*, R.A. 1815, oil on canvas, 155.5 × 232 cm, National Gallery, London.

69: J.M.W. Turner, *The Decline of the Carthaginian Empire — Rome being determined on the Overthrow of her Hated Rival, demanded from her such Terms as might either force her into War, or ruin her by Compliance: the Enervated Carthaginians, in their Anxiety for Peace, consented to give up even their Arms and their Children*, R.A. 1817, oil on canvas, 170 × 238.5 cm, Clore Gallery for the Turner Collection, London.

71: J.M.W. Turner, *Crook of Lune, looking towards Hornby Castle*, c. 1817, watercolour, 28 × 41.7 cm, Courtauld Institute of Art, University of London.

73: J.M.W. Turner, *A First Rate taking in stores*, 1818, watercolour, 28.6 × 39.7 cm, Cecil Higgins Art Gallery, Bedford, U.K.

75: J.M.W. Turner, *England: Richmond Hill on the Prince Regent's Birthday*, R.A. 1819, oil on canvas, 180 × 334.5 cm, Clore Gallery for the Turner Collection, London.

77: J.M.W. Turner, *MARXBOURG and BRUGBERG on the RHINE*, 1820, watercolour, 29.1 × 45.8 cm, British Museum, London.

79: J.M.W. Turner, *Dover Castle*, 1822, watercolour, 43.2 × 62.9 cm, Museum of Fine Arts, Boston, Mass.

81: J.M.W. Turner, *The Storm (Shipwreck)*, 1823, watercolour, 43.4 × 63.2 cm, British Museum, London.

83: J.M.W. Turner, *Rye, Sussex*, c. 1823, watercolour, 14.5 × 22.7 cm, National Museum of Wales, Cardiff.

85: J.M.W. Turner, *The Battle of Trafalgar*, 1822–24, oil on canvas, 259 × 365.8 cm, National Maritime Museum, Greenwich, U.K.

87: J.M.W. Turner, *Portsmouth*, c. 1825, watercolour, 16 × 24 cm, Clore Gallery for the Turner Collection, London.

89: J.M.W. Turner, *Prudhoe Castle, Northumberland*, c. 1825, watercolour, 29.2 × 40.8 cm, British Museum, London.

91: J.M.W. Turner, *Forum Romanum, for Mr Soane's Museum*, R.A. 1826, oil on canvas, 145.5 × 237.5 cm, Clore Gallery for the Turner Collection, London.

93: J.M.W. Turner, *Mortlake Terrace, the Seat of William Moffatt, Esq. Summer's Evening*, R.A. 1827, oil on canvas, 92 × 122 cm, National Gallery of Art, Washington, D.C.

95: J.M.W. Turner, *Petworth Park: Tillington Church in the Distance*, c. 1828, oil on canvas, 64.5 × 145.5 cm, Clore Gallery for the Turner Collection, London.

97: J.M.W. Turner, *Ulysses deriding Polyphemus — Homer's Odyssey*, R.A. 1829, oil on canvas, 132.5 × 203 cm, National Gallery, London.

99: J.M.W. Turner, *Scio (Fontana de Melek, Mehmet Pasha)*, c. 1832, vignette watercolour, size unknown, Private Collection.

101: J.M.W. Turner, *Loch Coriskin*, c. 1832, watercolour, 8.9 × 14.3 cm, National Gallery of Scotland, Edinburgh.

103: J.M.W. Turner, *Mouth of the Seine, Quille-Bouef*, R.A. 1833, oil on canvas, 91.5 × 123.2 cm, Fundaçao Calouste Gulbenkian, Lisbon, Portugal.

105: J.M.W. Turner, *The Golden Bough*, R.A. 1834, oil on canvas, 104 × 163.5 cm, Clore Gallery for the Turner Collection, London.

107: J.M.W. Turner, *Venice, from the Porch of Madonna della Salute*, R.A. 1835, oil on canvas, 91.4 × 122 cm, Metropolitan Museum of Art, New York.

109: J.M.W. Turner, *The Burning of the Houses of Lords and Commons, 16th October 1834*, B.I. 1835, oil on canvas, 92 × 123 cm, The Philadelphia Museum of Art, Philadelphia, Penn.

111: J.M.W. Turner, *Flint Castle, North Wales*, c. 1835, watercolour, 26.5 × 39.1 cm, Private Collection, U.K.

113: J.M.W. Turner, *Snow storm, Avalanche and Inundation — a Scene in the Upper Part of Val d'Aouste, Piedmont*, R.A. 1837, oil on canvas, 91.5 × 122.5 cm, Art Institute of Chicago, Illinois.

115: J.M.W. Turner, *Modern Italy — The Pifferari*, R.A. 1838, oil on canvas, 92.5 × 123 cm, Art Gallery and Museum, Glasgow, U.K.

117: J.M.W. Turner, *The Fighting 'Temeraire', tugged to her Last Berth to be broken up, 1838*, R.A. 1839, oil on canvas, 91 × 122 cm, National Gallery, London.

119: J.M.W. Turner, *Ancient Rome: Agrippina landing with the Ashes of Germanicus. The Triumphal Bridge and Palace of the Caesars restored*, R.A. 1839, oil on canvas, 91.5 × 122 cm, Clore Gallery for the Turner Collection, London.

121: J.M.W. Turner, *Venice: A storm in the Piazzetta*, c. 1840, watercolour, 21.9 × 32.1 cm, National Gallery of Scotland, Edinburgh, U.K.

123: J.M.W. Turner, *Slavers throwing overboard the Dead and Dying — Typhon coming on*, R.A. 1840, oil on canvas, 91 × 138 cm, Museum of Fine Arts, Boston, Mass.

125: J.M.W. Turner, *Snow Storm — Steam-Boat off a Harbour's Mouth making Signals in Shallow Water, and going by the Lead. The Author was in this Storm on the Night the Ariel left Harwich*, R.A. 1842, 91.5 × 122 cm, Clore Gallery for the Turner Collection, London.

127: J.M.W. Turner, *Rain, Steam and Speed — the Great Western Railway*, R.A. 1844, oil on canvas, 91 × 122 cm, National Gallery, London.

129: J.M.W. Turner, *Lake Lucerne: the Bay of Uri from above Brunnen*, 1842, watercolour, 29.8 × 45.7 cm, Private Collection, U.S.A.

131: J.M.W. Turner, *The Lake of Geneva with the Dent d'Oche: tending the vines*, 1841, watercolour, 22.8 × 29.1 cm, Clore Gallery for the

Turner Collection, London.

133: J.M.W. Turner, *Montreux, c.* 1841, watercolour, 23.4 × 33 cm, Clore Gallery for the Turner Collection, London.

135: J.M.W. Turner, *The Devil's Bridge, St Gotthard, c.* 1843, watercolour, 23.8 × 30.5 cm, Fitzwilliam Museum, Cambridge.

137: J.M.W. Turner, *The Falls of the Clyde, c.* 1844–46, oil on canvas, 89 × 119.5 cm, Lady Lever Art Gallery, Port Sunlight, U.K.

139: J.M.W. Turner, *Yacht approaching the Coast, c.* 1845–50, oil on canvas, 102 × 142 cm, Clore Gallery for the Turner Collection, London.

PHOTOGRAPH CREDITS